MAO ZEDONG

Anne Faulkner

FRANKLIN WATTS
LONDON • SYDNEY

Maps Ian Thompson
Designer Steve Prosser
Editor Emma Johnson
Art Director Jonathan Hair
Editor-in-Chief John C. Miles
Picture Research Susan Mennell

Consultant Eileen Yeo
Professor of Social and Cultural
History, University of Strathclyde

First published in 2003
by Franklin Watts
96 Leonard Street
London
EC2A 4XD

Franklin Watts Australia
45-51 Huntley Street
Alexandria
NSW 2015

ISBN 0 7496 4695 0

A CIP catalogue record
for this book is available
from the British Library.

Printed in Hong Kong/China

Picture credits
Front and back cover images: Topham

Associated Press/Xinhua p.50
Peter Newark's Historical Pictures
pp. 5, 21, 23, 29, 32, 35, 40, 43, 44,
47, 61, 65, 69, 72, 74, 77, 81, 89, 91,
105
Popperfoto pp. 13, 19, 38, 70, 79,
82, 85, 93, 96 (Andrew Wong/
Reuters), 102
Topham Picturepoint pp. 2, 3, 8, 16,
25, 53, 55, 58, 66, 87 (Associated
Press), 94, 99

Mao Zedong
1893–1976

Contents

Introduction

Mao Zedong (1893–1976) helped found the Chinese Communist Party and rose with it to power. As leader of the party, he transformed his country into the People's Republic of China, and was head of state from 1949 until his death.

Mao was the eldest son of a farmer in Hunan province. He was expected to take over the family farm, but he was determined to become a scholar and he succeeded. At 24 he left school and got a job in the university library at Beijing.

This was a turning point in Mao's life; China was in chaos and many new political theories were being tried out. In 1921, Mao became one of the 13 people who set up the Chinese Communist Party.

In 1927, after a few years of uneasy alliance, the republican Nationalists fought a long and bitter war with the Communists. In 1935, Mao was one of the military leaders on the Long March, the communist retreat from Jiangxi in the south to Shaanxi in the northern borderlands. Several of Mao's children died or were left behind. As a survivor, Mao built a power base within the party. Ruthless and manipulative, Mao soon got rid of his political enemies. In 1949, he proclaimed the new People's Republic of China with himself as leader.

To hold on to power, Mao kept China in a state of constant revolution until his death in 1976. During the 1960s, he became known in the west, mostly through the *Little Red Book*, his collected writings.

Chinese names and spellings

Chinese is a language made up of pictograms. It is quite difficult to translate them into English letter sounds and, to make things even more complicated, there are two systems of translation in common use (see p 107). To be consistent, we have used the more modern "pinyin" spellings throughout this book.

In Chinese, people's names are given with the surname first, followed by the given name. So "Mao" is a family name.

▶ *An image of Mao Zedong from a Chinese poster.*

Young Mao

Nothing in his birth or early life indicated that Mao Zedong would one day become the leader of his country.

Mao was not born into wealth, nor even an important family or city. Like his heroes, Napoleon Bonaparte and the Emperor Han Gaozu, he came from obscurity and rose to great fame.

Mao Zedong was born on 26 December 1893 in the village of Shaoshan Chung in Hunan province. Seven children were born to the family, and Mao was the eldest of the three sons who survived. His brothers were called Zemin and Zetan. The family were peasant farmers but by no means poor. Mao's father, Mao Shunsheng, had served in the imperial army, where he had earned enough money to buy 15 Chinese acres (about 1.2 hectares/3 acres) of farmland and could afford to pay a hired labourer. He also earned money as an agent by selling the rice and pigs raised by his fellow villagers. Mao's mother, Wen Qimei, came from the city of Xiangxiang, in a neighbouring district. She was a Buddhist, and Mao seems to have loved her as much as he disliked his father.

An angry young man

Mao and his father were always arguing. This was partly because they were as stubborn as each other and neither would give in. It was also because young Mao hated authority figures; his early life is littered with quarrels and resentment against teachers or leaders of any kind. Later in his life it would appear that while Mao hated authority figures, he had no argument with becoming one himself.

Mao's rebellious nature first showed itself when his father took him to work in the family rice fields when he was six years old. It was not unusual for Chinese children of this age to help out on the family farm – it still isn't – but Mao resented it, and said so. He wanted to be a scholar. When he was eight years old, his father sent him to the village school, but only to learn the basics so that Mao could keep the family's accounts. Like the other pupils, young Mao learned to read and write, and was taught the philosophy of the great Chinese philosopher Confucius.

The class had to learn the *Analects* (a collection of the writings of Confucius) by heart. Mao did not enjoy this, although he was hardly the only pupil to find it boring. He did not get on with his teacher, who was elderly and strict. What Mao liked best was reading. He was especially keen on two books very popular in China, *The Water Margin* and *The Romance of the Three Kingdoms*. They were historical novels, but Mao believed that they were historical fact, and argued fiercely with anyone who said that they were not.

A master manipulator

Mao soon learned how to play off his two "enemies". When he wanted to get out of school, he would claim that he was needed on the farm. He would do this when his father had gone to the local town, so that he could not be questioned. If his father asked him to work extra hours in the field, Mao would say that he had school work to do. Then he would find a secluded spot somewhere on the farm and settle down comfortably to read and re-read his favourite books.

Father and son continued to quarrel, with things getting particularly difficult when Mao reached the age of 13. He was a tall, strong boy, and

Confucius

Confucius (Kong Fuzi), or Master Kong (551–474 BC) was China's greatest traditional philosopher. He was a teacher and civil servant in his home state of Lu. Many people, rich and poor, studied with him, learning ritual, poetry, music and other arts. Confucian thought formed the basis of the Chinese education system for centuries.

Confucian values included veneration for parents and ancestors, and obedience to authority and hierarchy. Mao hated Confucianism. He (and many others at the time) saw it as an old-fashioned system unsuited to life in the 20th century.

not afraid of his father physically. One day, after yet another quarrel, Mao walked out of the house threatening to throw himself in the river unless his father apologized. His father said he would only do so if Mao knelt before him. Mao would only bend one knee. Finally his father apologized.

▲ *A view of Mao's birthplace at Shaoshan Chung in the province of Hunan.*

Early marriage

When Mao was 14, his parents thought that he might settle down and become less unruly if he got married. It was not unusual among Chinese peasant farmers to marry young and it brought advantages to everybody – although not always to the bride. Mao's mother, who was not very strong and who had no daughters of her own, would have a daughter-in-law to help around the house. Regardless of his age, Mao would be thought of as an adult, and could work full-time on the farm. This pleased his father, who had just acquired some more land and would not have to pay for a second hired hand to work it. Mao himself was pleased because he would no longer have to go to the village school.

So, in 1908, a bride was found. Not much is known about her. In fact, she died before she turned 21. She came from the Luo family and was a distant relative – her grandmother and Mao's grandfather (on his mother's side) were brother and sister. She may have been called Li and was some four or five years older than Mao. There were no children from the marriage and in later life Mao claimed that it had never been consummated.

Now Mao was married, he worked full time on the farm and kept the books for the family business. Yet he still wanted to be a scholar, much to his father's annoyance. They quarrelled as fiercely as ever, but Mao worked hard on the farm and did all

Kang Youwei and Liang Qichao

Important figures in the conservative reform movement at the beginning of the 20th century, the political theorists Kang Youwei and Liang Qichao, teacher and pupil, were the first that Mao Zedong came across. Kang Youwei (1858–1927) was educated in the traditional Chinese way, but rebelled and turned against the idea that emperors enjoyed a "Mandate from Heaven", and could therefore rule unopposed. In 1894 he started a study group "The Society of Studying How to Strengthen the Nation", and was joined by Liang Qichao (1873–1929), his pupil.

They discussed modern ideas such as democracy and the idea of a constitutional monarchy, in which the emperor would be answerable to his government. In 1898, Kang met the young emperor Guangxu, who was impressed with his ideas. They began a programme of reform, but were stopped by the Dowager Empress Cixi, who imprisoned her nephew for the rest of his life (he died in 1908) and ruled in his stead. Kang and Liang fled into exile, where they stayed until the establishment of the Chinese republic.

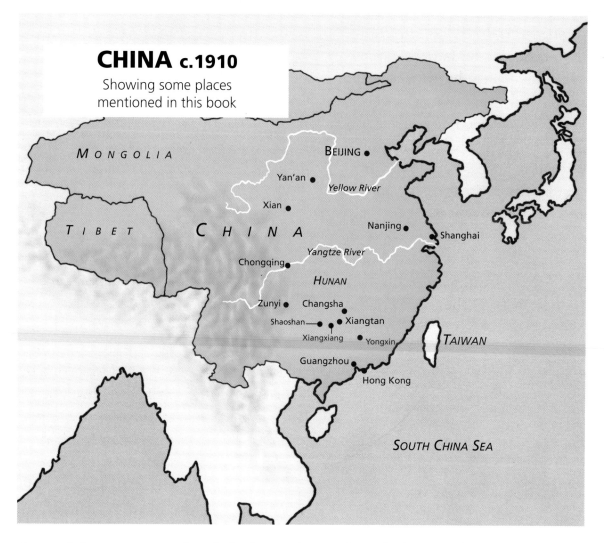

CHINA c.1910

Showing some places
mentioned in this book

MONGOLIA

BEIJING

Yan'an

Yellow River

Xian

TIBET

CHINA

Nanjing

Shanghai

Yangtze River

Chongqing

HUNAN

Zunyi

Changsha

Shaoshan

Xiangtan

Xiangxiang

Yongxin

TAIWAN

Guangzhou

Hong Kong

SOUTH CHINA SEA

the work he was supposed to do before opening a book. First of all, he studied with a young law student who lived in the nearby town of Xiangtan. Later, an older scholar called Mao Lu Chung (not related to the family) taught him classics and composition. More significantly, he introduced Mao to the writings of the political thinkers, Kang Youwei and Liang Qichao. For the first time, Mao came across politics and affairs outside his village. He decided to leave Shaoshan and go to school.

A determined scholar

Mao knew that his father would try to stop him, because he was needed on the farm. So he borrowed money from relatives and friends to pay for his school fees and hired a labourer to work in his place. In 1910 he left home and walked to Xiangxiang, about 24 km (15 miles) away, where he enrolled as a boarder at the Dongshan Primary School. It was not a success. At 16, Mao was three years older than the other boys at the school. He was almost 1.8 m (6 ft) in height, dressed in rough clothes and was awkward and abrupt in his manners.

Although good at classics and composition, Mao was not competent at maths, geography or languages. And he still fought with his teachers. For example, he was still convinced that the stories told in his two favourite books were historical fact. When one of his teachers tried to point out that they were just stories, Mao tried to bully his fellow pupils into signing a petition to get the teacher dismissed. He failed, but not before frightening the smaller boys.

Still Mao did not give up. When he found out that the teacher was a distant relative of the head of the school, he tried bullying tactics again – this time to force the head to resign. He failed, and left the school in less than a year. School did, however, introduce him to a wider world and he read Chinese translations of the biographies of Peter the Great, Napoleon and George Washington.

New education

Some Chinese leaders realized that the country would not keep up in the world unless it accepted new methods, scientific thought and technology. As the imperial system slowly collapsed in China, "foreign" ways of doing things were tried out. Ideas came from Japan, Russia and Europe.

One of the institutions to be changed was education. New schools were introduced following the European system of primary and secondary levels. That was why Mao had to go to a primary school first – even though he was far too old – before he could be accepted into the secondary level.

Mao the student

Undeterred by his experience, as stubborn yet insecure as he was to be all his life, the young Mao set off for Changsha, the capital of Hunan province, 48 km (30 miles) north of Xiangxiang.

In 1911, Mao enrolled in the Changsha branch of Xiangxiang Middle School. He paid 1,400 coppers (about £1.50 [$2.00] in today's money) for five months' board and equipment. Once again he was an average student. His calligraphy, a core subject of the Chinese curriculum, was considered clumsy, although his poetry and composition were praised and his reading improved. After about six months at the school, he ran out of money, and had to leave.

An introduction to politics

Changsha was a much more sophisticated place than the villages and country towns the young Mao had seen so far, and it gave him a glimpse of new possibilities. During his time at the school, Mao began reading a newspaper, *Ming Li Pao* (*The People's News*), published by the Tungmenghui, the predecessor of the Guomindang, the Nationalist Party. The paper supported the Nationalist leader Sun Zhongshan, and encouraged opponents of the corrupt Manchu regime to cut off their pigtails in protest. Mao immediately did so, and persuaded fellow students to do the same – in some cases forcibly cutting off their hair himself.

Mao was so impressed by the thoughts and writings of Sun Zhongshan that he wrote an article arguing that his hero should be the first president of China, with the political theorists Kang Yuwei and Liang Qichao as prime minister and foreign minister. He transferred this article on to a wall poster, which he distributed around the city.

This was probably the very first political poster in China. Young Mao noticed the impact it had, and

▶ *The nationalist leader Sun Zhongshan, photographed in 1907.*

remembered the power of the poster in later years, when he used it to great effect in his propaganda for the Chinese Communist Party.

It was also while he was at school that Mao heard a speech from a member of the Revolutionary Alliance, urging people to support the military mutiny which had begun in Wuhan, in an attempt to establish a republic.

Inspired, Mao decided to join the revolutionary army. However, he did not do so immediately, partly because it was the rainy season, and he did not have waterproof shoes. A few weeks later, the rebels were victorious and the revolution came to Changsha. The original leaders of the mutiny, Jiao Defeng and Chen Zuoxin, proved too revolutionary for their superiors and were killed by a sudden "mutiny" of their own troops. Mao saw their corpses lying on the street. It was his first lesson in power politics.

Considering the student volunteer army to be too badly organized, and in need of money, Mao decided to join the regular army, now officially the military arm of the Republic of China. He could read and write, he was big and strong, and his father had been a soldier. He used his army pay (around $8 Chinese a month) to buy books, magazines and newspapers, luxuries he had not been able to afford before. Perhaps more importantly, he found out what it was like to be looked up to and respected.

His fellow soldiers were mostly illiterate peasants, and young Mao used to write their letters home for them, and fill in their forms. He became their spokesman. He began to pay others to fetch water for him, although he was perfectly able to do it himself. Although of the people, it seems he now considered himself above such peasant tasks. Soldier Mao never saw action and left the army after six months to go back to his books and to continue his studies.

Success at last

At first Mao went back to the Middle School, but could not afford to stay. So he moved to a cheap hostel and worked out a programme for himself involving reading and studying every day, all day, at the public library. Here he read influential western works, including *On the Origin of Species* by Charles Darwin, *The Wealth of Nations* by Adam Smith and works by the philosophers John Stuart Mill, Jean-Jacques Rousseau and Herbert Spencer. These had all been translated into Chinese and, under the new Republican regime, were available in all major Chinese libraries. He also took a great interest in world maps. Mao Zedong spent most of 1912 following this self-imposed regime.

Back in Shaoshan, Mao Shunsheng was mortified that his son had no profession, bringing shame on the family. Although by all accounts very tight-fisted, he offered to help with tuition fees if Mao would sign up for a school and get some recognizable qualification. After considering accountancy and the law, the young Mao decided that he would become a teacher. In the spring of 1913, he enrolled at Hunan Provincial Fourth Normal School, which combined secondary education with a teacher-training course.

At long last, the scholar's life began to live up to his expectations. The school was modern, and taught western as well as traditional subjects. The curriculum was thorough. His fellow students were bright and politically aware, and Mao made friends. He got on with his teachers, who were some of the best scholars in the country, and his talents were appreciated. This did not stop him organizing a student strike in 1915, however, to protest against a rise in fees, for which he was almost expelled.

One teacher in particular was to have a profound effect on young Mao.

Yang Changji

Born in Changsha in 1870, Yang was a great intellectual, who had studied in Japan, Great Britain and Germany as well as his home country. His approach to teaching combined traditional Confucianism with western philosophy. He also believed that scholars should be tough physically as well as mentally and recommended vigorous exercise, hiking and swimming as valuable aids to clear thinking. Mao was very impressed with these ideas, and took up physical exercise himself. His very first published article, "On the effect of physical exercise", came out in the radical monthly magazine *New Youth* (*Hsin Ching Nien*) in April 1917.

This was Yang Changji (1870–1919), who taught ethics and social science and who came to the school in the same year that Mao enrolled. He was also known as Ch'en chi. He described Mao as his "third best student" and invited him, along with a handful of fellow students, to his home for meals and discussions. It was here that Mao met Yang's daughter Kaihui (1901–37) whom he was later to marry.

Studying and physical exercise did not distract Mao from political activity. With fellow students he set up a workers' evening school, teaching basic reading and writing skills (with some history and politics thrown in) for free. In school, he was heavily involved in the Students' Association. He negotiated the right to student self-government, gaining student representation on the school board and a say in the appointment of new staff. He became extremely popular with his fellow students, who voted him the "most outstanding figure in their midst" in June 1917.

◀ *A view of "Mao's well" in the courtyard at Hunan Provincial Fourth Normal School, where Mao enrolled in 1913.*

Mao's heroes

The young Mao was particularly impressed by people who had made it to the top from humble beginnings like his own. One of his heroes was the populist leader Li Zicheng (1605–45), who rallied millions of peasants to capture the imperial city of Beijing and in 1642 drove the Ming emperor Chung Chen to hang himself.

Another was Liu Bang or Liu Pang, who ruled as emperor Han Gaozu (256–195 BC), founder of the Western or Former Han Dynasty. He was the first ruler of China who had been born a peasant and was a great success. Under him China expanded into Korea and Central Asia, fought off marauding Huns, and at the same time produced great art and literature.

Later the same year Mao showed his grasp of military tactics when defeated troops of a northern warlord threatened the First Normal School with invasion. He organized armed policemen and students with toy guns and firecrackers in such a convincing way that the troops retreated. He was much praised and gained a reputation that extended beyond the school gates.

In June 1918, Mao Zedong graduated with honours. He was 24 years old.

B ckground to revolution

Mao Zedong was born just before the start of the 20th century, into a country that found itself shocked by the changes beginning to undermine its imperial society.

On one side Japan and Russia were hungry to expand their territories, on the other was the increasing power and influence of the west. Throughout Mao's childhood great changes were taking place in the way his country was governed. By 1911, when he was just reaching manhood, the country that had been ruled by emperors for millennia had declared itself a republic. The old order had been destroyed, but no one really knew what would replace it.

The decline of an empire

The Qing Dynasty, established in 1644, was the last to rule China. Qing emperors were known as the Manchus, because they came originally from Manchuria, a province in the far northeast of China. Their regime began to falter seriously in the second half of the 19th century. They maintained a life of luxury funded by political corruption in Beijing, while famine and floods killed thousands in the countryside. This led to resentment and anti-imperial feelings. At the same time, the Manchu court was faced with foreign aggression and rebellion at home. The huge military costs of dealing with these events meant heavier taxation, which led to more unrest throughout the country.

The two Opium Wars (1839–42 and 1857–60) with Britain resulted in humiliating defeat for China. Britain (and other western nations) gained 15 treaty (trading) ports, and the

▶ *This Chinese peasant farmer, photographed in 1905, is an example of the lowest level of the old order soon to be swept away by revolution.*

The Opium Wars

The two confrontations known as the Opium Wars were fought between Great Britain and China. Britain wanted to force the Chinese to accept opium (brought from India) in exchange for tea, porcelain and silk.

The second war (1857–60), in which Britain fought in alliance with France, was a result of the Chinese refusal to abide by the treaties signed to end the first war (1839–42). Under the Treaty of Nanjing (1842), Britain gained Hong Kong as a colony and five other treaty ports. During the second war, the Chinese were forced to sign the Treaty of Tianjin (1858) granting ten more ports to European powers and opening up the Yangtze River to foreign shipping.

territory of Hong Kong. The Manchu court thought that granting such concessions would be an easy way to hold off their enemies. Only too late did they realize it had opened the door to new ideas from outside the country, and so helped to encourage and influence the Chinese revolution that was to come.

Between the wars, the Manchu regime had to deal with the Taiping Revolt, the first serious and lasting challenge to its exclusive power.

Eventually (but only after 15 years) the revolt was put down, but the reforms it had introduced to southern China had long-lasting influence.

After defeating the Taiping rebels, the Manchu, under the guidance of the formidable Empress Cixi (1835–1908) tried to claw back its lost power and glory, and resist reform at all costs. However, more concessions were made to western powers (Britain, France, Germany, Spain, Portugal and the USA) and the country was defeated in two disastrous wars – against the French (1884–5) and the Japanese (1894–5) – which saw the destruction of China's new state-of-the-art navy.

The Chinese were divided on the question of reform. Some welcomed it, believing that only with western technical know-how would they be able to compete with the Japanese. Others suspected that foreigners wanted to exploit China's vast natural resources. In the 1870s, some attempt had been made to understand western ways, and scholars were sent to Europe and the USA. They came back with ideas about constitutional monarchy, democracy and republicanism.

▲ *Violent and bloody fighting took place during the Boxer Rebellion as multi-national troops battled with rebels besieging the Legation Quarter in Beijing.*

The final attempt to hold back the tide came with the Boxer Uprising of 1899–1900. This marked one last stand against foreign influence and it was backed by Empress Cixi. It failed and as a result China was forced to pay enormous amounts in compensation and grant even more concessions to the eight foreign powers that it had antagonized. Foreign influence became even more widespread.

The Boxer Uprising

Boxers was the name given to the hundreds of small, anti-foreigner secret societies that sprang up in China to fight against foreign influence and what they saw as exploitation. In 1899, supported by the Dowager Empress Cixi, they banded together and besieged the Legation Quarter of Beijing. This was where all the foreign embassies were and where most foreigners lived. During the siege hundreds of foreigners and Christians were killed. After 50 days the uprising was ended by a multi-national force of eight foreign powers.

As the Qing Dynasty was obviously declining, China reverted to its ancient power pattern – the might of the warlords. Powerful leaders, usually bandits, emerged to take advantage of the power vacuum left where central authority broke up. The ordinary people were caught in the crossfire between rival bands. Some warlords paid lip service to the emperor, but ruled their individual patch in their own way. By the time Empress Cixi died in 1908, leaving the two-year-old Xuan Zang as China's last emperor, Manchu power was broken and the country was ready for a new direction.

A Chinese Republic

The drive towards republicanism was led by Sun Zhongshan, a fierce opponent of the Manchu regime. He coordinated protests when he founded the United League, and after the death of Empress Cixi, helped organize revolts in southern China. He enjoyed popular support from the army and the middle classes, which believed that the imperial leadership had been weak

Sun Zhongshan (1866–1925)

Like Mao, the leader of the republican movement, Sun (in the old style Sun Yat Sen) was born a peasant, in the southern Treaty Port of Guangzhou. His family converted to Christianity, and Sun went to a Christian school, where he received a good education. His anti-imperial ideas made it sensible for him to leave the country. He trained as a doctor in Hawaii and Hong Kong and travelled in Japan, the USA and Europe to spread the anti-Manchu message.

On his return he founded the Revive China movement and the United League (Tungmenghui), to bring together different groups who wanted to see China strong again. This was the basis for the Guomingdang, the Nationalist Party founded by Sun Zhongshan. After the republic got off to a shaky start in 1912, Sun, who had no military back-up, allowed Yuan Shikai to take over the leadership. The Nationalist capital was moved from Nanjing to Beijing. Yuan soon reverted to his warlord habits, turned against democracy, outlawed the Guomingdang, exiled Sun and declared himself emperor. However, he died suddenly in 1916, leaving Sun to reorganize the party and get back on the republican track.

▲ *The 16 delegates of the Chinese Nationalist Party assembled in Beijing in 1911.*

and had led the country to defeat and exploitation. Not everyone agreed with Sun's ideas, especially the ruling classes, and he spent much of his time abroad or in foreign territories such as Hong Kong, Macao and Shanghai. In October 1911, rebellion was sparked by a military mutiny in Wuhan. Sun was in the USA, and had to rush back to support the movement. It became known as the Double Ten Revolt (tenth day of the tenth month), and so ready was the country for change that by 1 January of the following year, delegates from 16 provinces had elected Sun provisional president of the new Republic of China.

Beijing and the birth of communism

In June 1918 the newly qualified Mao found himself unemployed, like many of his colleagues, at a time of great political upheaval in his own country and abroad.

In the west, World War One was coming to an end, and Russia had just been turned upside down by a revolution that brought in a whole new political system. China was a republic in name, but drifting towards anarchy. The next three years were to bring enormous changes in Mao's life, which set him on the path to leadership.

In September 1918, Mao set off for Beijing, the first time he had ever travelled outside his home province. His old tutor, Yang Changji, was a professor at the National University there, and he used his influence to get Mao a job in the library. It was not a high-powered position – Mao dusted the shelves, swept the floor and checked out books – and it paid $8 Chinese a month, just enough for him to share a cramped three-roomed flat with seven other students. However, it allowed him to study, attend lectures and meet the intellectuals who were shaping China's future. Two of these, Li Dazhao and Chen Duxiu, became very important in Mao's life and the development of the Chinese Communist Party. As a lowly library assistant, Mao felt that the university staff and students looked down on him and that he was going nowhere. He had also fallen in love with Yang Kaihui, Professor Yang's daughter, and it is

▶ *Mao photographed in Beijing in 1918. At this point he was working as a library assistant at the National University.*

possible that the professor disapproved of the romance.

Six months after his arrival in the capital, Mao left. At home, his mother was ill, and the local warlord, General Zhang Jingyao, was acting in an oppressive way. On 14 March 1919, Mao arrived in Shanghai, where he said goodbye to many of his friends from the Work Study Programme who were travelling to Europe. He arrived home on 6 April and took a job teaching history at the Changsha primary and middle school, where he stayed until December. While he was away from Beijing, a student rebellion broke out – on 4 May – that triggered a fresh outburst of political dissent.

Mao the journalist

Unable to be at the heart of the new revolution, Mao decided that the best thing he could do was to keep Changsha up to date with events and new ideas. He established a journal, *The Xiang River Review* (*Xiangkiang Ping Lun*), which he wrote, edited and distributed almost single-handedly. The first issue of 2,000 copies sold out in a day, and by the last issue (of four) the readership had increased to 5,000. Mao's first editorial, very much influenced by the writing of

---

The Work Study Programme

In 1918, just as World War One was coming to an end, the Work Study Programme was set up by Cai Yuanpei, the Rector of Beijing University and his opposite number at the Sino-French University of Beijing. The plan was to sponsor Chinese students to travel to France where they would work in factories to fund their studies at French universities. Many of Mao's schoolmates went from Changsha, as did future political leaders such as Zhou Enlai and Deng Xiaoping. Although a keen supporter of the programme, Mao did not take up the opportunity. This was partly because he could not afford it and partly because he was very bad at languages (his attempts to learn Russian and English were failures). However, his friends wrote to him from overseas, and much of what Mao learned about the Russian Revolution came from the letters of an old friend Cai Hesen (1890–1931). Important Russian texts had been translated into French much earlier than they were into Chinese.

Li Dazhao, urged his readers to rethink every aspect of the old order – religion, politics, society, economics and education – and suggested that boycotts, strikes and mass peaceful protest were the way forward. He supported the idea of unions as a way for the masses to make their presence felt.

General Zhang soon closed the journal down, and Mao took over the editorship of the journal of the Xiang Medical School, *The New Hunan*. Again he promoted reform and opposed authority. So General Zhang closed down *The New Hunan* too. But Mao didn't give up. He found another newspaper to contribute to – the established Changsha newspaper, *Dagongbao*. His first article opposed the unfair treatment of women, criticized arranged marriages and supported equal civil rights for all Chinese women.

Mao actively carried out his political theories. In December 1919, he organized a 13,000-strong student strike against Zhang's repressive educational policies, which were starving schools of funding. The strike was harshly suppressed – Zhang sent his troops into schools to beat up any opposition – and

The Guomindang

The Guomindang is the Chinese Nationalist Party. It was founded in 1919 by Sun Zhongshan as the ruling party of the new Republic of China. After Sun Zhongshan's death, Jiang Jieshi took over leadership of the Party. Today it is still the ruling party in Taiwan, but known in the old style as the Kuomintang (KMT).

Mao became a marked man. His mother had died in October, so there was not much to keep him in Changsha. He went back to Beijing to visit the Yangs and drum up support to continue the fight against Zhang.

A tiny blossom of Marxism

Mao's second stay in Beijing was no longer than his first. Professor Yang died in January 1920, as did Mao's father. Mao did not return for his father's funeral but stayed on in Beijing to help the Yang family. He also got to know Li Dazhao better and was among the first to see Li's early versions of a translation of *The Communist Manifesto*. In April Mao was in Shanghai, where he met up with others from his home province of Hunan. They had been driven out of Hunan by General Zhang. Mao made contact again with Chen Duxiu, the revolutionary intellectual, and from him learned a great deal about the Russian revolution and Marxist theory.

Suddenly, and unexpectedly, General Zhang was deposed by a rival military alliance, and it became safe for Mao to go back to Hunan province again. He returned to Changsha in June, and was offered the job as director of the

Zhang Jingyao

General Zhang was a bandit from the north who became a military leader. He was imposed on Hunan as governor in 1918 by the republican Beijing government following a war in which thousands of Hunanese were killed or ruined. He did not improve his popularity by bringing his three brothers with him and giving them positions of power, smuggling opium and selling off mining rights illegally.

Zhang led a harsh, corrupt regime, which was hated and opposed by many, making it easy for Mao to organize mass protest and spread the communist message. In the summer of 1920 General Zhang was removed in a sudden coup, directed by Beijing-based General Wu Peifu (1874–1939), and a local, General Tan Yenkai, who was installed as governor.

Changsha Normal Primary School. He was considered a hero because of his constant fight against General Zhang. He was also under secret orders from Chen. In May 1920, Chen had set up the Provisional Central Committee of the Chinese Communist Party, appointing himself secretary. When Mao left for Changsha, Chen entrusted him secretly to spread Marxist ideas and find supporters in his home province. Back in Hunan, Mao's energies quickly found new direction.

The independent bookseller

In 1920, Mao set up the Cultural Book Society in Changsha. Its aim was to bring all the new political ideas directly to Hunan. In Mao's own words, they were to encourage "the growth of the tiny blossom of new culture that has appeared in Russia". The Book Society was to be a collective, funded by investors (including Mao himself), who would neither claim their money back nor demand dividends. There was to be

▶ *Karl Marx (1818–83), who wrote* The Communist Manifesto. *His ideas inspired communist leaders worldwide.*

The *New Youth Review*

Founded by Chen Duxiu in 1915, and co-edited by Li Dazhao, the *New Youth Review* (*Xin Qingnian*) was a forum for radical and revolutionary ideas, including the rejection of Confucianism. The review appealed to Chinese intellectuals, desperate to find a new way forward for their country. Li's essay in the October 1918 issue – entitled "The Victory of Bolshevism and approving of the new order in Russia" – had a great effect on Mao. The magazine also discussed new ideas, from Einstein to the emancipation of women. There were many other radical magazines at the time, but the *New Youth Review* was the most influential.

a book club so that those less wealthy could rent books to read. Backers included Li Dazhao and Mao's student girlfriend Tao Li. Mao sold books by western political thinkers as well as Chinese revolutionaries and stocked radical journals such as the Beijing-based *New Youth Review*. The venture was a success. Soon there were seven branches in county towns, outlets in schools and a string of home-based booksellers who sold books to their friends. In his private life, things were also going well for Mao Zedong. Yang

Kaihui returned to Changsha and she and Mao began living together as husband and wife.

Meanwhile, Mao was working hard supporting the cause of Hunan independence. This was very popular with local business people and merchants as well as the new provincial governor General Tan Yenkai. At this time, Mao believed that if each of the Chinese provinces achieved independence, the country would flourish as a federation – a kind of United States of China. In November 1920, Hunan province did declare its independence. A constitution was drafted that included civil rights for women. But without the right to set its own laws, government of the province was soon in the hands of warlord-led factions once more.

Mao used his existing network of small groups to spread Marxist ideas. The New People's Study Society, which he originally founded in 1914, was flourishing once again. He also set up various small study groups, based on Li Dazhao's Marxist Study Group, which usually combined discussion with picnics or walking tours. The aim was to promote Marxism and counteract anarchism, another popular political theory. Mao realized that small groups worked better for his purposes – he could control them more easily, and they would not attract the attention of the authorities. They were also easily set against each other if necessary.

Mao's political skills were improving rapidly. By the spring of 1921, the Hunan Branch of the Chinese Communist Party had been established.

The New People's Study Society

In 1914 the young Mao had set up the New People's Study Society (Hsin Min Hsueh Hui) with idealistic fellow students in Changsha. The warlord Yuan Shikai had declared himself emperor and China was in confusion. Young Chinese people wanted to find a new direction for their country. The aims of the original society were to encourage good moral conduct, exchange knowledge and ideas and foster friendships.

In 1918, supported by Mao's mentor Yang Changji, the society was re-launched on a more formal basis. When Mao came back to Changsha in 1920, he re-activated the group, with himself as leader. It was a perfect way to meet and vet people before inviting them to join the new Communist Party.

There were ten members, including Mao himself, all from the New People's Study Society.

The beginnings of Chinese communism

In March 1919, the Russian communist leader Lenin established the Third International – known as the Comintern. This was the theoretical basis for global communism, the spread of revolution and the rise and unification of the world's proletariat (industrial working classes). In 1920, Comintern agents arrived in China and contacted Li Dazhao and Chen Duxiu, the best-known supporters of Marxism.

In August, the first communist group was established in Shanghai. In November, the group produced a manifesto – much the same as the Russian version – and decided that its first priority was to organize the class struggle in various key areas. For this it needed the muscle, economic power and enthusiasm of workers, peasants, soldiers and students. Six cities were chosen as strategic centres – Shanghai, Beijing, Wuhan, Jinan, Guangzhou and Changsha.

It was not until the following April that Comintern agents returned to China with money to help set up the Chinese Communist Party. The First Congress of the Chinese Communist Party was officially called on 23 July 1921. Fifteen people attended the congress – two Comintern agents, and 13 Chinese. Mao was one of two delegates invited from Changsha. Li Dazhao and Chen Duxiu were not present, but included as founder members.

There was fierce debate and the Chinese delegates were by no means convinced that Russian communism was suitable for China, nor that they should take orders from Lenin. Eventually agreement was reached about how to proceed and spread the communist message. The main aim was to increase party membership and so the first priority would be to organize factory workers. Rules were established. If there were more than five party members anywhere in China they could form a society (soviet). Once a soviet contained more than 30 members, they could appoint an executive committee. Finances, party policy and publications would come from the Central Committee, with Chen Duxiu as General Secretary. The growth of the party was to be kept a secret until it was strong enough to declare itself.

Mao returned to Changsha, with instructions to build up the party in Hunan. He set up the Hunan Self-Study University with his fellow communist delegate He Shuheng. This was not a communist organization – it was funded by the province – but gave Mao the opportunity to sound out and recruit possible sympathizers. Marxist-Leninist theory was taught as well as other new international ideas, and it was open to anyone who wanted to learn. In November 1921 the Central Committee ordered Mao to recruit 20 new comrades. It is probable that Yang Kaihui joined at this time, as did Mao's younger brother Zemin. Mao also approached workers, successfully recruiting carpenters and construction workers he met on the building site of the new university.

In October 1922 Mao and Kaihui had their first child, a son whom they called Anying. Mao had committed to family life and a new political order.

◀ *A photograph dating from 1920 of the Russian revolutionary and communist leader Vladimir Lenin (1870–1924).*

Communists and nationalists

As the Chinese Communist Party grew, Mao grew with it. To begin with, the communists and nationalists were uneasy allies, forming a United Front against the invading Japanese.

But the alliance soon crumbled. Bitter civil war raged on and off until 1949, punctuated by ceasefires and attempts at peace between 1936 and throughout World War Two (1939–45). It was during this period that Mao rose to national fame as one of the leaders of the Long March (see p 46) and the cult of Maoism began to take hold.

Uneasy alliance

Mao was a founder member of the Chinese Communist Party in 1921. He spent the following year or so in Changsha helping to set up worker associations, organizing strikes, and trying to recruit more members and attract more support. However, things were not moving fast enough for Russia, now led by Stalin. He was funding the Chinese movement and it was still very small. The Russians wanted the Chinese communists to form an alliance with the Guomindang (Nationalist Party) led by Sun Zhongshan, in an effort to attract more members and achieve some power in the country. Many Chinese communists, including Mao Zedong and Chen Duxiu, one of the founders of the party, objected to

Communist Party membership

The Communist Party in China grew from a very tiny seed. When it was established in 1921 there were only 53 members. A year later, there were 195. In 1923, there were 420, ten of whom were in prison. By 1925, there were still fewer than 1,000, but by spring 1927, numbers had swollen to 57,000.

▲ Mao as a founder member of the Chinese
Communist Party. This photograph of him looking
self-assured dates from the early 1920s. At this stage
the party had fewer than 1,000 members.

this. The nationalists had different aims. They also co-operated with the USA, the northern warlords and politicians friendly to Japan. But the Russians insisted – and since they provided the money, objections were ignored. In August 1922, it became compulsory for all Chinese communists to join the Guomindang. But it was not until spring 1923, rather later than his superiors in the Communist Party, that Mao finally joined the Guomindang.

Personal and political problems

Mao's political career came into conflict with his personal life. At the Third Congress of the Chinese Communist Party, held in Guangzhou in 1923, Mao was elected to the Central Executive Committee, which ruled the party, and was made head of the organization department. He was working in Guangzhou and Shanghai at a time when his home province of Hunan was in the grip of a reactionary new military leader who was closing down schools and suppressing unions. Yang Kaihui was living in Changsha

where in November 1923 she gave birth to the couple's second son, Anqing. She was unhappy that Mao could not be with his family.

Mao was also uneasy about his political position. With others, including Chen Duxiu, he put forward a formal protest to Stalin about the increasingly powerful right wing of the Guomindang. He no longer wanted a "United States of China" – he thought it would be nothing but an uncooperative collection of provinces dominated by warlords. He was beginning to think that a political ideology without military force to back it up was unlikely to succeed.

Peasants and military power

For a year, between December 1924 and October 1925, Mao dropped out of the political scene altogether and returned to his home province. Several reasons have been put forward about why he did this – family ties, a return to his roots, perhaps a desire to keep out of arguments about the Nationalist-

Communist alliance. In any event, he went back to the peasants of Hunan, whose lives, work and thinking he understood. He organized night schools where they could be taught to read and write, and learn the rudiments of Marxism. He began developing his ideas on land reform (taking the land away from the people who owned it and redistributing it fairly among the people who worked it) and the setting up of co-operative peasant associations. He became convinced that no social change would succeed if the peasants were not included as part of it, and that rural activism (making the peasants politically aware, and giving them basic military training) was essential.

In 1925, Mao returned to public life, apparently a dedicated follower of the party line, and began work on Guomindang propaganda in Guangzhou. His work with the Hunan peasants was recognized, and between May and September he was made director of teaching at the Peasant Movement Training Institute. In February, he had slipped back to Hunan for two weeks to check how the peasant movement was progressing, but now he was able to work openly. A fact-finding mission to Xiangtan district produced detailed notes on every aspect of rural existence, and was the first of three important documents written by him describing peasant life.

The 1927 coup

Despite the death in 1925 of Sun Zhongshan (leader of the Guomindang) from cancer, the United Front appeared to be holding. The two parties had set up a joint military academy in Whampoa, under the direction of the nationalist, Jiang Jieshi (Chiang Kai Shek), with communist Zhou Enlai as deputy head. In 1926, the combined armies (led by Jiang) launched the Northern Expedition, an operation planned to break up individual military-led regimes and unify the country.

However, in 1927, the United Front crumbled. In March, the Northern Expeditionary Force took Shanghai and a quarrel broke out over who should control the city.

▲ This picture shows a conference at the Whampoa academy in 1924 prior to the start of the Northern Expedition. Jiang Jieshi is on the left and Sun Zhongshan in the middle, with Madam Sun on the right.

Jiang Jieshi and the right wing of the Guomindang made an alliance with northern warlords and staged a coup in April of that year. Jiang's Nationalist troops killed thousands in Shanghai and the communist movement there was destroyed.

Chinese communists wanted to break with the nationalists, but Stalin insisted that they continue to work with the left wing of the Guomindang. A base for the communist left-wing Guomindang Alliance was set up at Wuhan, and Mao was sent there, taking with him the Peasant Movement Training Institute. By the summer the left-wing nationalists had decided to join Jiang Jieshi's right wing and abandon the communists.

The final break came with the Nanchang Uprising on 1 August 1927, which ended in disaster for the communists. Led by Zhou Enlai, with military commanders Zhu De, He Lon and He Ying, the communists took the city and set up a 25-man revolutionary committee. But without backing from the people, their action failed. Mao attended an emergency meeting of the Communist Party at Hankou, during which Chen Duxiu was deposed, the alliance with the nationalists was declared over, and the communist troops were reborn as the Red Army. The Chinese communists were independent at last but they found themselves under attack on all sides from provincial warlords and the nationalists.

The wilderness years

Mao and his peasant supporters were now trapped in eastern Hunan. The party leadership ordered him to encourage the peasants to rebel, but he realized that they would need more organization as well as the support of communist troops to have any impact. In October, after forming an alliance with some bandit leaders, he retreated to Jinggangshan, in the remote Jinggang Mountains on the border of Hunan and Jiangxi provinces. Now he was cut off from the party and from his family (Kaihai had just given birth to their third child, Anlong).

▲ A formal portrait of General Jiang Jieshi. Jiang became leader of the Guomindang. Defeated eventually by the communists, he was exiled to the island of Taiwan..

In 1928, Mao was stripped of all his party titles. He met He Zizhen, the 19-year-old daughter of a prominent communist family from the nearby town of Yongxin, and began a relationship with her. Their first child, a girl, would be born in January 1929.

Jiang Jieshi

Known in the old style as Chiang Kai Shek, Jiang (1887–1975) was born the son of a merchant in Zheijiang. He was sent to Japan for his military education but returned in 1911 to join the revolution to overthrow the Manchu Empire. In 1918, Jiang joined Sun Zhongshan's revolutionary government and became Commandant of the Whampoa Military Academy.

After Sun's death in 1925, Jiang became the leader of the Guomindang and was nationalist president of China from 1928–31 and again from 1943–49. He established the nationalist capital at Nanjing. After 1927, Jiang led the right wing of the Guomindang in a civil war against the communists. After years of struggle, Jiang Jieshi was beaten and exiled to the island of Taiwan, where he led an authoritarian, anti-communist regime backed by the USA.

Mao was now the leader of a group of about 10,000 peasants and soldiers – mostly troops from the remnants of the Red Army, who had found Mao's hideaway as they fled from the nationalists. To keep the group together, Mao imposed a number of rules, which were harsh but fair. Land was distributed equally, and everyone (except the sick, the very young and the old) had to work their share. Soldiers received land but peasants were paid to work it while the troops were fighting. Everybody paid land tax. The troops were badly equipped but what they had was shared equally so no one could complain. It was in this hideaway that Mao began to put to good use his guerrilla warfare tactics. Most of these he had learned from the ancient Chinese classic on military strategy, *The Art of War* by Sun Tzu, or from the old historical romances he loved to read.

In January 1929, Mao decided to move his group to a new base to escape constant attacks and find more food and supplies. They found a new site on the border between

Jiangxi and Fujian provinces, which was known as the Jiangxi Soviet. The move brought Mao back into the party circle. He was once again under party instructions – and criticism, especially of his guerrilla tactics. However, he was appointed Chairman of the Provisional Soviet Area Government.

Mao's lowest ebb

Life in Jiangxi was pretty miserable. It had not been a good move strategically, because it was under heavy attack from Jiang and the nationalists. Despite his relationship with He Zizhen, Mao missed Yang Kaihui and his sons, still living in Changsha. But he was never to see Kaihui again. In October 1930, after a failed attack on Changsha, she was arrested by Guomindang troops, and shot when she refused to renounce Mao or communism.

In 1932, the Japanese attacked Shanghai and took over Manchuria, putting the last Chinese emperor, Henry Puyi, on the throne. About this time, He Zizhen gave birth to a son, Anhong, but Mao had fallen

Guerrilla tactics: *The Art of War*

The Red Army was scattered and had little equipment and less food. Mao realized that there was no point trying to fight in a traditional way against the larger, stronger nationalist army and the mercenaries who fought for the warlords. He needed guerrilla ("little war") tactics.

He studied *The Art of War*, written in the fourth century BC by Sun Tzu, which set out the advantages of espionage, informants, deception, psychological warfare, sabotage, knowing your terrain and understanding the enemy.

Mao's troops learned to fight only when they had superior numbers, how to move by stealth, how to lure the enemy into their territory and pick them off, how to capture a base, establish local support and then move on. Mao adapted four of Sun Tzu's rules, and made them into simple slogans for his soldiers:

- When the enemy advances, we retreat
- When the enemy halts and makes camp, we trouble them
- When the enemy seeks to avoid battle, we attack
- When the enemy retreats, we pursue

▶ *Invading Japanese troops march through a village in Manchuria in 1932.*

▲ An early coloured photograph of Mao addressing a communist conference in 1933. At this point the Japanese advance had forced the Chinese Communist Party to move its headquarters to Jiangxi.

Mao's children

Mao had ten children in all, with three different partners. Four died in infancy and two disappeared. Mao's first arranged marriage produced no children. With Yang Kaihui, he had three sons, Anying, Anqing and Anlong. After their mother was shot, in 1930, the children went to stay with friends of the family in Shanghai. The youngest child died there, but Anying and Anqing were sent to the Soviet Union in 1936.

With He Zizhen, Mao had a daughter in 1929, who died in Fujian. A son, Anhong, was born in 1932. He stayed behind with Mao's younger brother Zetan when the Long March began, but disappeared after Zetan was killed in 1935. A third child, born in 1933, died in infancy. During the Long March, Zizhen gave birth to a daughter, who had to be left behind with a peasant family, and was never found again. In 1936 another daughter, Li Min, was born. She survived, grew to adulthood and had children of her own. In 1938, He Zizhen went to the USSR where she gave birth to another child who died after a few months.

Mao's last official partner, Jiang Qing, gave birth to his last child, a daughter Li Na, in 1940.

---

ill. For two years he suffered from malaria, TB and other diseases.

Politically, Mao was almost destroyed. Although the Japanese invasion of 1932 led to more people joining the Communist Party in protest, it also meant that party headquarters had to move from Shanghai to Jiangxi. Mao found himself sidelined in his own soviet. He was excluded from top level meetings, and denied a place in the Central Politburo (the committee in charge of setting out party policy). At the same time, the arrival of a group of Chinese scholars who had trained in Russia meant that policy reflected what the Soviet Union thought best for China. Mao and others were beginning to realize that Chinese communism would not work if it followed the Russian model.

Meanwhile, Jiang Jieshi and the Guomindang army had surrounded Jianxi, putting the communists under siege. In October 1934, the party leaders decided to abandon the base. What happened next – the Long March – would establish Mao as a leader of the party.

The Long March

Now regarded as the most important event in the history of communist China, the Long March (Changzheng) was a disaster when it happened.

The march lasted a year and covered 9,660 km (6,000 miles). Thousands were killed or died along the way of disease, starvation or exhaustion. At the beginning Mao was simply another fleeing communist, but by the end he had become a person of great power.

Breaking out

On 18 October 1934, Mao and He Zizhen joined the exodus of around 86,000 heading for western Hunan. The marchers were mostly men – Red Army troops and party members. Nearly all the women stayed behind, except the wives or partners of some of the leaders. Mao begged for He Zizhen to be allowed to come with him, and the couple had to leave their little boy behind with Mao's brother. They never saw the child again. Around 15,000 troops stayed behind to defend the sick and wounded.

The marchers had no transport, except for a few horses and pack mules. The troops were carrying all their weapons, including heavy artillery. Party members carried all their paperwork as well as heavy machinery, which they hoped to reassemble when they found a new base. Most of this was thrown away along the route as it became impossible to carry.

After a battle at Haienfeng, the marchers burst through the nationalist lines and began their escape. They covered about 40 km (25 miles) a day, but they often had to march through the night to escape bombardment from the air.

The marchers were attacked mercilessly as they tried to cross the Xiang River in Guangxi province.

▶ *A view of the Long March in 1934–35, showing communist forces struggling over a ridge in the Great Snowy Mountains.*

Jiang Jieshi's troops bombarded them from the land and air. It took a week to get across, and by this time almost half the marchers were killed or wounded. Many deserted. Once across the river they carried on, unsure of where they were going. At the city of Zunyi, the leaders stopped to re-think their plans.

The Zunyi conference

The march reached Zunyi on 5 January. The next day, the party held a conference called the Enlarged Meeting of the Politburo. It lasted for two days. The 17 people who attended, including Mao, discussed the failure of the defensive military tactics at Jiangxi (see p 45). There was also criticism of the Jiangxi failure to support an attempted anti-nationalist rebellion in Fujian. Zhou Enlai's military tactics during the battles they had fought on the way were also criticized by various generals.

But the real disagreement was between Politburo members who supported the Russian party line, and those, like Mao, who thought the party should be free from Russian influence. It was a fight for leadership.

Eventually, the military leaders sided with Mao. Zhou Enlai realized that he had lost the military argument, and also sided with Mao. Mao was elected Chairman of the Politburo and, supported by Zhou Enlai, decided to move on to Shaanxi province in the far northern reaches of China.

On the move again

With Mao now leading one of the military columns (advised by Zhou), the marchers moved on. Various attempts to cross the Yangtze River failed, and they were forced to go far southwest before turning north, almost to the border with Tibet. They finally crossed the Yangtze at Zhou Bing Fort ferry, using Mao's favoured guerrilla methods – by night, after disguising themselves in Guomindang uniforms and easily defeated a small garrison of nationalists.

They were now in Sichuan province. Mao's leadership did not go unchallenged. Many military commanders opposed him and did not want to risk their troops protecting

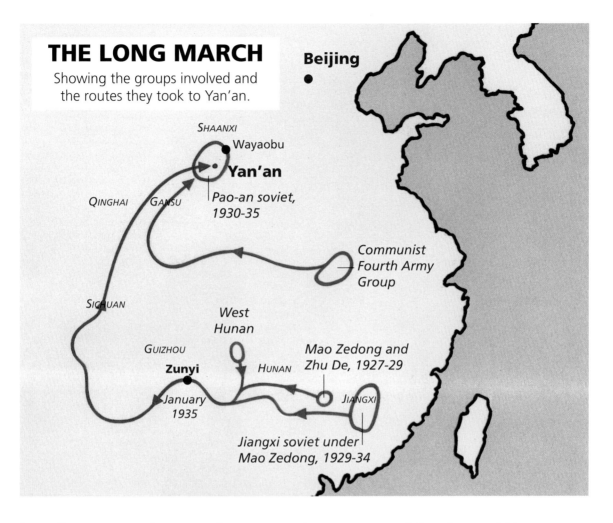

THE LONG MARCH

Showing the groups involved and the routes they took to Yan'an.

Beijing

SHAANXI
Wayaobu
Yan'an
Pao-an soviet, 1930-35

QINGHAI   *GANSU*

Communist Fourth Army Group

SICHUAN

West Hunan

GUIZHOU
Zunyi
January 1935

HUNAN

Mao Zedong and Zhu De, 1927-29

JIANGXI

Jiangxi soviet under Mao Zedong, 1929-34

him. Some set up their own bases. General Zhang Guodao, who had supported Mao at Zunyi, disagreed with him about the direction of the march, and took his troops, together with those of General Zhu De and marched eastwards. Mao was in command of about 15,000 men when the marchers began their nightmare journey across the swamps and mountains of Qinghai and Gansu. They had to eat berries and leaves, or risk being killed by local tribespeople if they tried to steal sheep to eat. It was freezing at night and damp in the daytime. Many died of malnutrition or poisoning but at least there were fewer nationalist attacks.

In October 1935, around 8,000 exhausted marchers arrived at the

village of Wayaobu, in Shaanxi province, where they met up with other communist troops who already had a base there. Mao had survived, physically and politically. Zhou Enlai had made it as well, despite being very ill on the march and carried on a stretcher for most of the way. He Zizhen had been badly wounded in a bombing raid. She had given birth to a daughter who had been left behind with a peasant family.

A new beginning

In the summer of 1936, the communists decided to make the market town of Yan'an their base. It was a walled market town, surrounded by sandstone hills. Local people had been carving cave shelters in these hills for centuries, and they made ideal homes for the communists who had few resources. Mao and He Zizhen lived in such a cave, with their new daughter Li Min. Mao had also had good news about his two surviving

◀ *A photograph taken at a communist base in Shaanxi province sometime between 1934 and 1936 shows, from left, Qin Bangxia, Zhou Enlai, Zhu De and Mao Zedong.*

Zhou Enlai

When the Long March began Zhou Enlai (1898–1976) had been the Chief Political Officer of the party, but he was ousted at the Zunyi conference. However, he did not oppose Mao, and the two worked together closely during the second half of the march.

Zhou had been a member of the Chinese Communist Party since it began in the 1920s. He was a moderate man, acting diplomatically to prevent damaging quarrels within the party. He acted as liaison officer between Mao and Jiang Jieshi, making good the damage of some of Mao's excesses.

Zhou was always loyal to Mao, and was one of the few people who never fell out of favour. He was Prime Minister of China from 1949 until his death.

sons, Anying and Anqing. They were alive, although Anqing was unwell. Zhang Guodao and Zhu De, the two generals who had quarrelled with Mao, finally arrived at the communist stronghold. They and their troops were exhausted and they were in no position to oppose Mao's increasing power.

In the relative safety of the new base, Mao turned his attention to strengthening the Communist Party. He also began his climb to the top of the party tree.

Winning the battle

Once in the relative safety of Yan'an, Mao began to build his own power base as leader of the party.

Mao agreed with his enemy Jiang Jieshi that "power comes from the barrel of a gun". He realized he would have to succeed on the military front as well as the political. As he saw it, his first task was to beat the nationalists. In this he was helped by Japan's aggressive invasion into Chinese territory, the outbreak of World War Two and, eventually, lucky geography.

Neutralizing the nationalists

Although two more divisions of communist troops finally made it to Yan'an, the Red Army was in no state for all-out war. Mao and Zhou Enlai decided instead to work on a propaganda campaign. Mao understood that the Chinese people could not comprehend why a civil war was being fought when the Japanese threat was so strong. Zhou organized the distribution of leaflets calling for an end to fighting among the Chinese and a renewal of the United Front against foreign aggressors. Many of these leaflets reached the nationalist

troops. One soldier who was influenced by them was General Zhang Xueliang, a former Manchurian warlord who had been driven out of his territory by the Japanese. Although an ally of Jiang Jieshi, he could not understand why he had to point his guns at the communists when only a few miles to the north, the Japanese were advancing. Zhou Enlai set up secret meetings with General Zhang to encourage his support of a United Front against Japan, and as a result the general decided not to attack Yan'an. This significant change of direction by Zhang led to the Xian Incident.

The Xian Incident

In December 1936, Jiang Jieshi flew into Xian, the main city of Shaanxi province, to urge his reluctant troops to finish off the Yan'an communist base. On 12 December, he was kidnapped, possibly on the orders of Zhang Xueliang, and held to ransom. General Zhang wanted Jiang Jieshi to agree to a United Front. Although it has never been made clear

▲ *This photograph of Mao creating a piece of calligraphy was taken in Yan'an in 1937.*

whether or not the communists were involved in the plot, the kidnapping was a gift to Mao, who had just been elected Chairman of the Communist Military Council.

The communists at last had their enemy in their power. They could have decided to execute Jiang. This was the option that Mao had wanted at first. Alternatively, they could hold on to him until they had won over the people with their planned reforms; they could release him on condition he withdrew his troops from Shaanxi province; or they could

force him to agree to a United Front against Japan.

After a debate, which proved fierce but brief, they agreed that it would be better for the communist cause if Jiang was released on certain conditions. These were: an immediate ceasefire; a peace conference at Nanjing, the nationalist stronghold; the formation of a United Front against Japan; nationalists and communists working together towards a unified China.

Jiang was released on Christmas Day, two weeks after his kidnap. The release gave Mao and the communists a political advantage. They could point out that the kidnap had been a nationalist incident, nothing to do with them. They made it clear that they were against the common Japanese enemy. And if Jiang refused to agree to a United Front, and civil war broke out again, the communists could with justification blame the nationalists.

Mao's gift for manipulation and propaganda brought the communists to national and international notice as a serious, patriotic political force. Jiang had to agree to a United Front, although in reality he was slow to take action. Not until July 1937 was he forced to move.

The struggle against the Japanese bought two advantages to the communists – the weakening of the nationalist army and a stream of new supporters. Most of the fighting was done by the nationalist army, which was almost destroyed in the process. In December 1937, the Japanese took Nanjing. The nationalists were forced to retreat along the Yangtze River to Chongqing. The Japanese followed them eastwards and, as they advanced, set up puppet states run by Chinese collaborators. People were forced either to live under these regimes or flee to the nationalist or communist strongholds. Tens of thousands of people chose to go to Yan'an, because Mao and his group were seen by many as the only hope against the enemy.

The United Front held throughout World War Two (1939–45), but there were still many times when nationalists and communists turned against each other in local battles.

The domestic scene

Mao was also making changes to his home life. One of the many communists who had come to Yan'an from Shanghai was Jiang Qing, a B-list actress. She was introduced to Mao by his Security Chief, Kang Sheng. He Zizhen was pregnant again, but still unwell from the wounds she had received during the Long March. She also suspected that Mao was no longer interested in her. In 1938, she left to go to hospital in Shanghai, but instead went to Moscow, since Shanghai was no longer safe. Mao sent on their daughter Li Min to stay with her.

In 1939, Jiang Qing moved in with Mao, sharing his two-roomed cave, and working as his personal secretary. When she became pregnant, she wanted Mao to

Jiang Qing

Born in Zucheng, Shandong Province, Jiang Qing (1914–91) began life as Li Yun-ho. She became an actress in Shanghai, working under the stage name of Lan Ping. In 1938, she joined the Communist Party, and so made her way to Yan'an with many other communists on the run from the Japanese.

During the early years of her partnership with Mao she had little political influence. In the 1960s, however, she played an important part in the Cultural Revolution, and was a member of the Politburo. She was one of the Gang of Four (see p100) arrested after Mao's death and sentenced to life imprisonment.

▲ Mao and Jiang Qing, the actress from Shanghai who became his fourth wife. The couple began sharing Mao's two-roomed cave in Yan'an during 1939.

JAPANESE EXPANSION INTO CHINA

Red areas indicate Japanese occupation up to 1941.

make their relationship official, but the Party leadership was opposed to this. He Zizhen was respected and liked, part of the circle of intellectual communist women, and a party activist from a respected communist family. She had been extremely loyal to Mao, losing five of her six children as a result of going with him on the Long March.

But Mao was determined to get his own way. In the end, the leadership allowed Mao and Jiang to live together as long as she had no political position. This showed that Mao was learning how to impose his will and obtain what he wanted in the face of opposition. The couple had a daughter, Li Na, in 1940.

An end to war

As early as 1942, Mao had correctly guessed which way World War Two would end. He thought that the long battle of Stalingrad (1942–43) had ruined Germany's chances of victory. He began to plan post-war tactics. He knew that the nationalists were planning to take over when Japan lost. But when the end of the war came, in 1945, no one in China was really prepared, and no one knew what the Americans and Russians were planning to do. The USA dropped atomic bombs on the Japanese cities of Hiroshima and Nagasaki on 6 and 9 August. On 8 August, the Soviet Union declared war on Japan, as agreed at the Yalta Conference, and Russian troops invaded Manchuria. On 15 August Japan surrendered.

This was where lucky geography came in. Mao's group, and other communist bases, were nearer the north and Manchuria than the nationalists were, and moved their troops in as soon as the surrender was announced. Mao wanted to get his hands on the area's rich resources

The Yalta Conference

This meeting was held in February 1945 at Yalta, in the Crimea (southern Russia). It was three months before Germany's final surrender, but the USA, USSR and UK met in secret to discuss what would happen when peace came. Among other things, they decided how Germany would be split up, and who would rule Poland. It was also agreed that the USSR would declare war on Japan three months after the Germans surrendered, which they did on 7 May 1945.

(minerals, including oil, and great forests) and establish a stronghold. Communist troops were helped by the Soviet army, who fought alongside them, passed on stockpiles of Japanese arms and equipment and ferried or airlifted Red Army troops to strategic positions. This helped to prepare the communists for the final struggle with the nationalists.

Even so, Mao was prepared to try a more peaceful path to national unity first. Late in August, he went to the heart of nationalist country – Chongqing – to meet Jiang Jieshi. The meetings were refereed by the US ambassador Patrick Hurley, and lasted until October. They agreed, in principle, to form a unified army and to call a Political Consultative Conference to discuss the future of the country. So little progress was made over the following months that in 1946, US President Harry S Truman sent George Marshall to restart the talks. The communist demands were: a democratically elected coalition government; communists to receive the surrender of Japanese if it happened in their own areas; political prisoners to be released; traitors to be punished.

Birth of a new republic

The talks got nowhere and fighting broke out in Manchuria. At first the nationalists did well, and in 1947, captured the Yan'an base. But the communists had withdrawn from it weeks earlier and settled in more northerly bases. From this reasonably safe area, Mao planned a brilliant counter-offensive, once again using guerrilla tactics. The campaign, launched in September 1947 was extremely successful. It was helped by the attitude of most Chinese people, who had become sick of fighting and were tired of the harsh punishment the nationalists inflicted on dissenters. The country was also in a state of financial chaos after World War Two. Within a year, the

Soviet bounty

When Soviet troops invaded Manchuria to finish off the Japanese, they passed on weapons and equipment that had been stockpiled or captured to the communists. This helped equip the Red Army for the struggle to come with the nationalists. According to sources at the time, the Russians passed on:

- 740,000 rifles
- 18,000 machine guns
- 800 aircraft
- 4,000 artillery pieces

nationalist army was driven from Manchuria. The Red Army advanced southwards, and during 1949, Beijing, Nanjing, Shanghai and Changsha fell to communist forces. By October, Jiang Jieshi and his troops were surrounded and trapped in Guangzhou. The nationalists were beaten.

On 1 October 1949, in Beijing, Mao announced the formation of the People's Republic of China, with himself as President.

◀ *Beijing residents salute as communist forces enter the city in 1949 following the defeat of the nationalists. Mao's portrait is in the centre on the wall.*

The rise and rise of Mao and Maoism

While Mao masterminded military strategies, he was also plotting the political moves that would eventually take him to the top.

Mao had already moved from a political unknown before the Long March to member of the Politburo and Commander of the military (as well as a member of the Seventh Comintern Congress) at its finish. Now he was aiming at complete control of the party. Over 13 years – from 1936 to 1949 – he used all his political skills, cunning and Hunan obstinacy to reach his goal.

The intellectual battle

Mao's military tactics may have been a success – and he was rapidly becoming a cult figure among his young followers – but he still had many opponents in the Communist Party. They accused him of having no political theory to back his actions, which was true. Unlike many of his colleagues, Mao had not been educated at university, had not travelled abroad to study, knew no languages and had not been able to read the works of Marx or Lenin in the original. He knew he was vulnerable, and so began to further his education by reading books on philosophy and economics and working out theories of his own.

It was Chen Boda (1904–89), who helped Mao defeat his intellectual enemies. A university professor and journalist, he came to Yan'an in 1937, fleeing from the Japanese. He helped Mao get a grip on the political theory behind the Russian Revolution and taught him how to fight intellectual battles with intellectual weapons. With his usual shrewdness, Mao realized what an asset

▲ From man to myth – Mao recognized the value of propaganda, and idealized images such as this one began to appear regularly in China after 1949. They promoted his image as a strong leader.

Chen was, and made him head of research in the Communist Propaganda Bureau as well as his Political Secretary in 1940. Chen wrote, or helped to write, most of Mao's speeches, articles and essays. He also created intellectual arguments that justified Mao's past tactics and helped him to formulate his own ideology. This ideology ultimately became known as Maoism.

Mao needed no help in discrediting his opponents in the party, and fighting against criticism from the ever-growing numbers of intellectuals who were arriving at Yan'an. He used all the political skills he had developed over the years, such as propaganda (what would today be called PR and "spin"), intimidation, fear, flattery, bribery, the spreading of rumours, manipulation and violence.

Building the image

Years before, Mao had understood the power of the poster and the flyer to spread information. So in June 1937 he allowed the first ever "official" picture of himself to be published. It appeared in *Liberation*, Yan'an's revolutionary newspaper. He and Zhou Enlai distributed leaflets and essays in the nationalist areas of China, targeting students. The communists were described as heroes undergoing great hardship, and it was implied that they had been marching north to confront the Japanese enemy. This explanation of the march spread throughout China and out into the world. The communists and their leaders (especially Mao) were seen in an heroic light. While Mao did not actively encourage a cult, he did not put a stop to it. Young admirers put together and published a collection of his short works late in 1937.

Mao also understood the importance of his image as a straight-talking man of the people. He was often seen tending his vegetable patch ("Mao grows his own food") and entertaining venerable peasants ("Mao respects his elders"). He always wore old patched clothes, and refused to move out of his cave into a house, saying that he did not want to have more privileges than the ordinary person. He stressed his peasant origins, using colourful, down-to-earth language and scratching his body for lice during political meetings. As a result he inspired loyalty and affection among the ordinary people, the kind of loyalty that political rivals recognized as a very potent weapon indeed.

The political animal

Behind the image of the strong, manly Mao was the political wizard. His party rivals were not so easily dazzled by his image, but he dealt with them like a chess master, always three or four moves ahead. He played jealous or ambitious rivals off against each other. He used divide-and-rule games, splitting up alliances and favouring one side or the other.

When a political rival proved tough, Mao used flattery and reward. One such rival was Wang Ming, the powerful Chinese delegate to the Third International – a direct line to Moscow. In 1937, Mao sent him to Hankow as part of a three-man delegation to meet with the nationalists, saying he was the best man for the job.

Mao was also very astute at choosing people who would do a good job while remaining loyal to him. Zhou Enlai remained loyal to Mao throughout his long career, and Mao could not have maintained such good relations with non-communists and the international scene without him. Kang Sheng, Mao's security chief, made sure that Mao knew about every whisper of intrigue and plot against him. Liu Shaoqi reorganized the party along Maoist lines, and remained Mao's loyal second-in-command until the Cultural Revolution (see p 86).

A secret force

Being a politician, Mao knew that ideology needed force to back it up. As military leader, he was in charge of Yan'an security. The base was at real risk from nationalist spies, and some sort of screening process was needed to vet all newcomers. In 1938, Mao and Kang Sheng, his head of security, began to build up a secret security force. Recruits were chosen very carefully and trained in the mechanics of the job by Kang, while Mao gave them lessons in ideology.

It seems that no one else knew about the force, although they were between 4,000 and 8,000 strong by 1942, when recruitment stopped. Mao now had the loyalty of the army to fight the enemy outside, and his own hand-picked, personally trained security force to fight against his enemies within.

Maoism

Maoism is a western term. It was known to his contemporaries as "Comrade Mao's Thought". In Mao's words his ideology was "Marxism adapted for Chinese circumstances". Where Marxism relied on the organization of the industrial working class, Maoism depended on organizing the peasants. It was Chen Boda who helped Mao to express this new ideology.

But that was not all. Mao had become very anti-intellectual, making a complete U-turn from the ideas of his youth. This may have been due to the behaviour of the arrogant theoretical communists who fled to the safety of Yan'an, but looked down on the peasants they found there. Mao may have had painful memories of how, earlier in his life, scholars had looked down on him when he was struggling to educate himself. Whatever the reason, Mao now seemed to view books and book learning as worthless. He thought that art and literature should reflect the ideas of the people, not stand above them or lift them to another level. Intellectuals were told to identify with the masses rather than instruct them.

The Rectification Programme

Once he had established an ideology, Mao was as inflexible and stubborn as ever and determined that everybody should follow his ideas. On 1 February 1942, he gave a lecture at the official opening of the Yan'an Party School, during which he outlined his thoughts.

Party intellectuals continued to question and criticize Mao's ideas. At first he tried to answer his critics, but this failed to silence them. Fearing that he would lose control, Mao introduced a programme of re-education. It was known as the *Cheng Feng* movement – the "Rectification of Work Style" – and became a ruthless, three-year purge of dissidents. Everyone had to go through the process – if they refused, they were punished. People had to reveal their past, their social background, their contacts and prove their loyalty by informing on someone else. Members were divided into small groups and forced to criticize themselves and each other and to apologize for "incorrect thinking". People were taught to interpret the past and look to the future only in Mao's terms. The secret security police ran the so-called re-education programme. Thousands were killed or committed suicide. This programme gave Mao complete control.

▶ *An early communist poster shows Mao as the strong father of a happy and hard-working people.*

在毛澤東的勝利旗幟下前進

In control of the party

By 1943, Mao held all the cards. He controlled the military, had built up a powerful popular image of himself, scattered his rivals and built up an inner circle of loyal support. Leaders who had once criticized him now found it practical to praise him. He became known as "the centre of all revolutionary history" and "Great Helmsman". He had silenced any criticism of his ideas.

In May 1943 he was given two new titles – Chairman of the Communist Central Committee and Chairman of the Politburo. The Comintern was dissolved, so Moscow no longer told Mao Zedong how to run things.

Now his supporters began to rewrite the history of the Communist Party. They put Mao at the centre, making his early contributions more significant than they had been and presenting all his actions in a favourable light. His enemies, past and present, were all shown to have been wrong. This revised version of historical events has made it difficult for modern historians to uncover all of the facts and piece together an objective picture of what really happened.

▲ An official portrait of Mao dating from 1945, the year that he consolidated his power and took overall control of the Chinese Communist Party.

In 1945, Mao's power was made supreme. He had successfully fought off a meeting of the Seventh Party Congress since the end of the Long March, because he knew that the decisions made at Zunyi might be overturned, and he would lose his place.

By postponing the Congress, he had given himself time to build up a firm base. By the time the Congress met, in April-June 1945, Mao was in complete control. He was leader of the Party and his own ideology formed the basis of party thought and policy. It was written into the Constitution: "The Chinese Communist Party takes Mao Zedong's thought – the thought that unites Marxist-Leninist theory and the practice of Chinese revolution – as the guide for all its work, and opposes all dogmatic or empiricist deviations."

The basic elements of Maoism

- The party to be organized on Marxist-Leninist lines – a centralist democracy in which party members select party officials, discipline party members and dictate party policy.
- Peasants and farming were to be the building blocks of a socialist society. In Marxist theory, socialism is seen as the transitional state between capitalism and communism. The aim of Maoism was the dictatorship of a rural rather than industrial proletariat (working class).
- Armed struggle as a form of revolutionary activity.
- Constant revolution to prevent the formation of new elite groups.

In power

When Mao stood on the rostrum at the top of the Tiananmen Gate on 1 October 1949 and declared China a People's Republic, he became the leader of 600 million people whose country was in chaos.

Mao had achieved his dream, but now he had to deliver. Only someone with his personality and character – tough, cunning, determined, convinced that his way was the right way – could have taken the helm at this point, and kept China on course.

Mao and the party faced huge problems. The country was weak after 40 years of war and fighting. There was financial chaos, with inflation and no national currency. Communications were collapsing – rail tracks were smashed, canals clogged and telephone lines broken. Schools and universities had no equipment and few staff, and many people were homeless or had been driven out of their home provinces. Everyone scrambled along doing what they had to do to survive and there was widespread theft and corruption. On the borders of the country – Tibet, Mongolia and Xinjiang, a Muslim area, people were agitating for independence. And the nationalists, banished to the island of Taiwan, were still a possible threat.

But one of Mao's beliefs was in the power of destruction. He now had a country in which all the old structures had been so thoroughly broken down that he was now in a position to build a new one on Maoist principles.

Mao and Stalin

In December 1949, Mao left China for the first time in his life to go to Moscow for a meeting with the Soviet leader Joseph Stalin. It was a one-to-one meeting, with only interpreters present. When he had been struggling for leadership in Yan'an, Mao had always appreciated Stalin's backing. Now he wanted his help. Stalin gave Mao 300 million US dollars' worth of aid, and help with development of air transport and the rebuilding of the Chinese navy. They discussed Maoism, and Stalin expressed an interest in Mao's written work. Mao

▲ Mao Zedong proclaims the founding of the People's Republic of China from the Tiananmen Gate in Beijing, 1 October 1949. China was in chaos and urgent action was needed to modernize the country.

▲ Mao and the Russian leader Joseph Stalin (right) meet in Moscow early in January 1950.

A boost from Stalin

In 1937, while Mao was in Yan'an, Moscow still had great influence on the leadership of the Chinese Communist Party. Stalin had sent a message, via Wang Ming, that he considered Mao to be the best man for the leadership. The Soviet leader thought that although weak on ideology, Mao was very experienced in the practical side of revolutionary struggle. Stalin's approval must have greatly improved Mao's status in the party.

became uncharacteristically modest, and said that he wanted to review his work before having it translated into Russian since it contained "errors". Mao had another meeting with Stalin that took place in January, but this time Chen Boda and Zhou Enlai were with him, and the meeting was much more formal and diplomatic. It was the last time Mao saw Stalin, who died in 1953.

Mao returned to Beijing to undertake the enormous task of building China anew. For this he used all of the skills and experience that he had acquired organizing peasant associations, the Jaanxi soviet and Yan'an. The party leadership moved quickly and the new order began to emerge.

Home life

Mao and Jiang Qing moved into a real house at last. The senior members of the party all had living quarters in Zhongnanghai, a group of old walled buildings near the Forbidden Palace in Beijing. Mao's two daughters lived with their father, and attended the local school. Mao's eldest son, Anying, lived and worked nearby. Anqing, the second son, also lived in Beijing. A pool was built so that Mao could swim, because he had loved swimming since he was a boy. All seemed to be going to plan, domestically and nationally, when the threat of war loomed once again.

War again

In March 1950, Mao discovered that Kim Il Sung, the communist leader of North Korea, was about to attack South Korea.

Troubleshooting

Mao moved quickly to establish the communist regime. These were some of his initiatives.
• Students and young members of the Communist Party were given crash courses in land reform and sent across the country to put it into practice.
• Regional government structures were set up, supervised by party officials, civil servants and military staff.
• New ministries were developed in Beijing to oversee defence and industrial development.
• School and college systems were re-built.
• All media were put under state control to ensure the correct ideological message was going out.
• The railway system was repaired and expanded.
• Plans to nationalize industrial plants were put into action.
• The civilian population was disarmed (because the war had been won).
• Counter-revolutionaries were pursued and sent to trial.

There was debate in the Communist Party. Mao wanted to support the North Koreans, partly because they were communists, partly because any war would be a threat to China's borders and partly because he thought it would be a useful propaganda tool. The Chinese

people would be encouraged to pull together in the face of the enemy, and this would further strengthen the Communist Party. Chinese victory would impress neighbouring countries. It would also offer a chance to hunt out any remaining nationalist sympathizers, spies or other opponents. Mao was also convinced, wrongly, that the USA would not support South Korea. His party colleagues were not so keen. They thought the country was not ready for yet more fighting, and wanted guarantees of Soviet support before sending troops to Korea. Mao won the argument and on 19 October 1950, the Chinese entered Korea. However, Mao paid a high price – just over a month later his son Anying was killed in the fighting.

Starting over

Reconstruction began again, after a war that had brought nothing to China but a climate of fear (created by the witch hunts for anti-communists and counter-revolutionaries). This atmosphere of fear only increased Mao's power.

◀ *A 1951 photograph shows Chinese troops marching through Shanghai on their way to Korea.*

Mao borrowed the Russian model of the Five Year Plan. Since industrial growth was of the utmost importance, workers were guaranteed an "iron rice bowl" in order to increase production. This meant they were virtually unsackable and were given subsidized food and housing, and free health care and education.

In the country, peasants' lives were heavily regulated. Those from poorer areas were unable to move around in search of work without permission. An equivalent of the industrial "work unit" was created in the peasant co-operative – a unit, usually based on an existing village, where land and equipment were shared and worked communally. The peasants supplied grain at below market price to the government to fill the industrial workers' rice bowls. At the same time, peasants were ordered to work in groups on large-scale building works such as canals, reservoirs and hillside terracing.

Barely half way through the Five Year Plan, Mao was becoming impatient. Progress was too slow for him. He wanted the peasant co-operatives to expand so that the food supply to the cities could be increased. With more radical re-organization, more land could be

worked, and private plots and informal farmers' markets closed down.

Other party members disagreed. They believed that individual successful peasants should be encouraged to increase their plots of land, and therefore their produce, so that the state could take the surplus. Mao accused his critics of "walking like women with bound feet" and of not wanting to progress. Either way, they could not win – if they were too keen to expand, they were accused of "leftist deviation", if they wanted to hold back, they were accused of "rightist deviation". Mao's way was the right way, and he was going to go ahead.

Mao in isolation

Mao was now an unstoppable force, isolated from any criticism, meaningful opposition or good advice from colleagues, friends or family. He was in overall charge of his country and of a party of five million members, yet was increasingly unaware of what was really happening, partly because people were too frightened to tell him. The media,

◄ Land reform in China's countryside included the burning of official records dating back to imperial times, such as here in 1951.

controlled by the party, dared not report the true statistics of the Five Year Plan's progress. The organization and bureaucracy of government were far too complex for one man to handle, and so Mao was bothered less and less by detail.

In the early 1950s, Mao had travelled widely around the country, revisiting Hunan and speaking directly to the people. Later in the decade he rode in his special train, surrounded by bodyguards and personal attendants. Once he wrote regularly to family members and old friends from his school and university days. Later, his personal secretaries and assistants dealt with all his correspondence. Both his brothers and his eldest son were dead, and by 1956, he no longer lived with Jiang Qing.

There was no one to moderate Mao's vision. Even though he often contradicted himself, he began to believe that his opinion was always correct. Those who risked speaking out were punished.

This state of affairs was the background to the two disastrous initiatives known as the "Hundred Flowers Movement" and the "Great Leap Forward" of 1957.

A Hundred Flowers and the Great Leap Forward

In the two years from 1957 to 1959, when he stepped down as Head of State – but continued to wield supreme power – Mao introduced two new ideas. Both had devastating consequences.

In February 1957 Mao gave a four-hour speech at the Supreme State Conference, attended by party members and specially chosen non-party intellectuals. It was a curious speech, more like "thinking out loud". Mao considered the contradictions in Chinese society, the conflicts between communists and non-communists and the arguments about "correct thinking" within the Party. He wondered if they were going about things the right way. Since 1952, when a "Thought Re-moulding" campaign had been launched to ensure everyone was sticking to the Maoist line, around 700,000 people had been killed as "enemies of the state". Yet, Mao noted, there was still dissatisfaction, there were still too few schools, some people did not

have enough to eat and so on. He suggested a way of solving problems, by letting "a hundred flowers bloom and a hundred schools of thought contend". People were encouraged to come forward with criticisms and suggestions for progress. New ideas could compete with each other and the best solutions found.

So intellectuals and critics spoke publicly about what they saw as shortcomings and suggested ways to solve the problems. The intellectuals who had been educated abroad spoke loudest in their criticism. But the "flowers" were chopped down almost immediately. In June, Deng Xiaoping, the Secretary General of the Communist Party

▶ *An official portrait of Mao from 1958 shows a robust, relaxed and happy leader.*

launched a critical counter-campaign. Those who had spoken up were stripped of their office and privileges and sent to labour camps in the country. Scientists, economists, writers and artists all suffered, but so, in the long term, did the country.

Craftily, Mao had lured his intellectual enemies into the open and cut them down in one efficient harvest. A lot of old scores were settled and he was able to show the intellectuals he resented that he was the boss. The scheme allowed other people to denounce enemies as well.

Deng Xiaoping

Born in Sichuan, Deng Xiaoping (1902–97) went to France when he was 16 on a Work Study Programme and joined the Chinese Communist Party while he was there. Deng met Mao in the Jaanxi soviet. He became a trusted colleague and in 1954 was made General Secretary of the Communist Party. His opposition to Mao's Great Leap Forward and collaboration with Liu Shaoqi made him a marked man.

During the Cultural Revolution he was persecuted and stripped of his job (but not his party membership). In 1974, he was restored as Vice Premier, but sacked again in 1976. Two years after Mao's death, Deng came back to power again, ruling China until his death.

Mao knew what hardship accused people were suffering – he even intervened a few times to prevent people he knew and liked from being banished. Even so, the Movement made most people too frightened to criticize any of his policies and allowed him to go on to his next campaign completely unopposed.

The Great Leap Forward

Mao had been urging the party to speed up agricultural and industrial progress. He wanted China to overtake Europe and the USA in production. He now thought that the Russian-style Five Year Plans were too slow. He wanted to expand existing peasant co-operatives into huge collective communes, run on the same lines regardless of local conditions. Bigger must mean better, he thought, which is curious when his own peasant background taught him otherwise. However, any economists or scientists who came up with uncomfortable facts that showed large communes or the digging and planting methods would not work had been banished or silenced. Mao ploughed on with his ambitious plan.

In February 1958, the Great Leap was launched at the National People's

▲ *The Great Leap Forward gathers momentum as workers make steel in a backyard furnace.*

Congress. No one dared object. Mao believed that the mixture of revolutionary fervour and sheer numbers would win out over expertise. So instead of new industrial plants, small steel-making furnaces were built in backyards, and fed with pots and pans and scrap metal. Mao called this "making steel by the whole people". Revolutionary workers were encouraged to take over factories.

By August, peasant co-operatives had been merged with communes to produce huge collectives, each run by a form of local government and protected by a militia. There were around 24,000 of them, including Mao's home village of Shaoshan. The land was owned by the state but worked by the peasants. Private life was all but abolished. There were communal canteens, laundries, nurseries and schools – to free women from their traditional roles and allow them to work in the factories. Barefoot doctors took care of any health problems.

Traditionally, most peasants, even when working for others, had kept their own vegetable patches or small plots to grow their own food, but now these were banned. Mao spoke of his vision at the party's annual summer retreat.

The policy was a disaster, but no one wanted to risk Chairman Mao's rage by saying so. Statistics and figures were falsified so that production appeared greater than it was and harvests appeared

Barefoot doctors

During the Great Leap Forward, peasants' health was in the hands of part-time local people trained in basic sanitation and medicine. Traditional Chinese medicine (herbalism and acupuncture) was used along with more modern methods. The peasant "doctors" did not wear shoes, which is how they got their name.

During the Cultural Revolution (see p 86) , many medical workers were sent to the country. Their job was, ". . . to promote and implement state hygiene principles and policies; administer the water works and sewage systems; make improvements in wells, toilets, livestock areas, stoves and environment; give vaccinations; control infectious diseases; collect information on epidemics; and provide simple medical treatment and temporary rescue."

bigger. The media made exaggerated claims about production levels. Very little usable steel came out of the backyard furnaces. In the collectives, peasants became more discontented as they worked to impossible schedules drawn up by incompetent leaders. Mao would accept no criticism of his policy and so the Leap continued.

Yet Mao had always been pragmatic, and at heart was a solid Hunan peasant. He must have known that, despite what he was being told, there were problems. In a party meeting held in Wuchang in November 1958, his comments showed that he knew about the danger of famine, the need to collect real data, the unrealistic quotas and the lies, evasions and incompetence. In December, a few minor modifications were introduced to the policy. More significantly, Mao resigned as head of state, handing over the leadership to Liu Shaoqi.

Stand off at Lushan

Just because he no longer held the title, it did not mean that Mao was not head of state in all but name. He was still Chairman of the Communist Party and had supreme political power. Stepping

"The joy of a bumper harvest." This propaganda poster shows happy and productive workers enjoying the benefits of their labours. In reality, Mao's agricultural policy was a disaster.

▲ Mao's vision for China was out of touch with reality as workers struggled to meet quotas.

This photograph shows agricultural workers trying to cultivate land beside an unimproved road.

Mao's vision

At the summer retreat in 1958, Mao outlined his vision of China after the Great Leap. So much food would be produced that no Chinese would have to pay for it, and the country could give away the surplus to the poor of the world. Clothes would be free and everyone would wear the same. Discipline and hard work would make everyone strong and healthy so that doctors would have nothing to do but medical research. Money would be unnecessary. Women would not be tied to domestic drudgery. There would be no need for private housing. China would be transformed into such a beautiful place that no one would need to travel in search of beauty. This vision tells us more about Mao's character and philosophy than economic reality.

down meant he could now concentrate on pushing forward with his Great Leap without losing face if it failed.

In July 1959 there was a Central Committee Conference at Lushan to discuss the Leap's progress. The defence Minister Peng Dehuai criticized the Great Leap in a letter written to Mao. Peng did no more than repeat Mao's own comments about the false data, the lack of hard information and the technical and economic incompetence in the industrial

work units and agricultural communes, but in rather stronger language. Mao chose to see this as an assault on his authority and his leadership of the Communist Party. He also used it as a political tool to make sure that the Great Leap continued.

He made copies of Peng's letter. At the final meeting of the conference he gave everyone a copy, which he forced them to discuss. He made a 40-minute speech denouncing Peng, then challenged the members of the Committee to choose between the two of them. Needless to say, Peng had no defenders. He was exiled to Sichuan under house arrest to "improve himself through political studies and self-criticism". With the party leadership once more under his thumb, Mao was again able to push forward his disastrous policy.

Famine took hold in 1960. The situation was made worse by the weather – terrible storms, droughts, floods and typhoons. Twenty million people died. Yet, on paper, because of falsified information, the peasants still produced a surplus of grain and this was taken from them, leaving the communes with no food. Peasants were moved off the land to work in factories. Urban communes were introduced, so that schools, factories and offices were now run on collective lines.

Retreat from disaster

In the spring of 1961, Mao at last allowed a proper critical review of his policy. This was partly as a result of the split between Soviet Russia and China. Premier Khrushchev withdrew Soviet advisors, equipment and funds. Mao ordered three seven-man teams to investigate three sample communes, one of them in Hunan. When all the teams had reported in, Mao's secretary gathered the information they had collected and drew up a list of recommendations. Then, Mao ordered a document to be drawn up, addressing the main problems.

Mao turned what ought to have been a humiliating retreat into political advantage. Having gathered an impressive collection of true facts and a realistic picture of the situation, he taunted other party leaders for not having the courage to do the same. Liu Shaoqi and others immediately made their own reviews, but were made to look as if they were simply following Mao's brave lead. However, as a result, sensible changes were made, most significantly the reduction of communes to a manageable and efficient size. It was the new leader, Liu Shaoqi, who pulled China out of the hole in which the Great Leap had landed the nation.

Mao meanwhile had sensed political danger elsewhere and was moving on to new intrigues. He did not forget who had opposed his Great Leap Forward. As usual, he was waiting for the ideal time to strike against his enemies.

The break with the USSR

After Stalin's death, the new Premier, Nikita Khrushchev, led the revolt against the dead leader's cult of personality. He also started a programme of "de-Stalinization", reversing many of Stalin's policies. Mao denounced Khrushchev's revisionism. He was worried that people would oppose his own personality cult. The bad relationship between Mao and Khrushchev led to tension. The Soviet Union demanded payment for the USSR's support during the Korean War; the Chinese believed it had been freely given.

In 1960, the Soviets removed staff and equipment from major Chinese projects, such as the atomic bomb programme and development of the oil fields. During the famine, the USSR offered a gift of free grain, but Mao refused it. There was a short border war in 1969, and tension continued between the two countries until Mao's death.

▲ A friendly meeting between Mao and Soviet leader Nikita Khrushchev in December 1962.

Behind the smiles a deep rift was developing that would lead to a border war in 1969.

Cultural Revolution

Although communism had brought about great changes, Mao was still not content. In the 1960s he launched the Cultural Revolution – a campaign to rid the country of traditional ways. Much of China's cultural heritage was seriously damaged.

Engineered by Mao, but from a distance, the Cultural Revolution reached its height in 1966 and 1967, but the after-effects continued until Mao's death in 1976. Millions died or watched their lives fall to pieces and Chinese art, literature and science were seriously damaged. There is no written record of Mao's aims or intentions for this campaign of upheaval.

Build-up to chaos

Why did Mao want to stir up trouble just when China was settling down into relative prosperity? After his retreat of 1959, and the moderation of the Great Leap Forward policy, Mao was feeling excluded from the frontline of power – even though it was his own decision to step down as head of state. Worse, the Thought of Chairman Mao – Mao's collected political ideology – was being downgraded. In 1956, it had been decided to drop it from the Communist Constitution as a mandatory requirement. The party felt that it encouraged the cult of personality, which had been Stalin's downfall. Mao had reluctantly given in to pressure and agreed to it being removed. Peng Dehuai had been one of the party members who urged the Thought to be taken out, and Mao exacted terrible revenge on him.

At the same time, Mao saw that fewer people were buying his works. This was partly due to a paper shortage. Priority was given to printing millions of new school books, which were greatly needed. Liu Shaoqi, appointed Head of State by Mao, ordered that the phrase "Thought of Mao" be removed from any propaganda designed for foreign consumption. And in 1960, the propaganda unit warned that Mao's Thought was being trivialized – it was being used to explain success in table tennis tournaments.

Mao was in danger of being stranded on the island of his own ideology. However, two major party figures – Minister of Defence Lin Biao and Security Chief Kang Sheng – decided to follow Mao rather than fall in with the party line. Perhaps they remembered what had happened to those who criticized Mao during the Hundred Flowers Movement, or perhaps they took a calculated risk on Mao's eventual victory. Kang Sheng's support was no surprise, because he had always been loyal to Mao. Lin Biao was hoping to be named as Mao's successor.

▲ *Mao enjoyed travelling in luxury. Here he works while flying on a private jet.*

Lin Biao's support was particularly important. He controlled the army, and Mao had always known that any campaign needed the support of the army to be successful. Lin wrote an enthusiastic piece about the 1961 edition of Mao's *Selected Works*. He said that victory in war was a victory for Mao's Thought: "Our present important task is to arm our minds with Mao Zedong's thought, to defend the purity of Marxist-Leninism and combat every form of ideological trend of modern revisionism."

Despite these two allies, Mao still felt insecure, and so he ordered a fact-finding mission, as he had done so often before, to collect ammunition against further criticism. His secretary Tian Jiaying went to Hunan (Mao always preferred to gather signs of the times from his home ground). Unfortunately, the information he collected was not what Mao wanted to hear. The peasants were happy about the modifications to the Great Leap, but they wanted even smaller working units. Many of them wanted an end to co-operative farming altogether. Mao's response was to say: "We want to follow the mass line but there are times when we cannot completely heed the masses."

To make matters worse, Liu Shaoqi and Deng Xiaoping wanted to return agricultural production to the small, one-farm unit. Mao was being outflanked politically and increasingly isolated.

Another reason for Mao's lack of popularity in the party was his decadent lifestyle. This was the man who had claimed that the simple cave life was all that a true revolutionary needed. Now he lived in luxury. He and Jiang Qing had stopped living together and nowadays he entertained a number of young women friends. He lived either in the Zhonghanghai complex at Beijing, in the various summer guesthouses in the country and along the coast, or he travelled in his luxurious private train.

Mao was 70 years old, feeling ignored and disempowered. His hard-won ideology was crumbling. He wanted to regain power and control, but he had few allies left. Mao was an obstinate Hunan peasant, but he was also a master politician. So he did what he was best at doing – he started a revolution. It happened slowly.

Behind the scenes

Mao genuinely believed in perpetual revolution and the creative power of destruction. He believed that "fires should be set" every few years to keep revolutionary fervour alight. He also knew that to have a successful revolution, you had to identify an enemy. He began to engineer a split in the party between the "truly Red" people who supported him and believed in the power of the masses, and those who believed in progress through expertise, knowledge and experience. These people were labelled bourgeois revisionists.

The Great Leap Forward had been based on agricultural and industrial theory. The new revolution would take place on the cultural battlefield. Mao still carried the anti-intellectual chip on his shoulder. Rightly or wrongly, he felt left out of the circles of cultured party members and made no secret of his loathing of them.

Mao already had one general on this battlefield – Jiang Qing. He had promised

▲ *Zhou Enlai remained Mao's trusted associate. This photograph shows the two men together in 1963.*

that she would not have political influence, but supported her interest in the arts. After she came back from Moscow in 1956, she was a given a minor post with a brief to encourage revolutionary art, writing and performance. This seemed a harmless activity to the other party leaders at the time. But now she was in a strong position to seek out those who agreed with Mao. She began a campaign to banish revisionism from the arts. At the same time, Kang Sheng began to look for proof that novels were encouraging anti-party activism.

Mao also knew that young, idealistic students were the foot soldiers of any revolution. In 1964, his nephew Mao Yuanxin became a student at the Harbin Institute of Military Engineering. His daughter Li Na studied history at Beijing University. Mao encouraged both of them, particularly Yuanxin, to report back to him on the level of revolutionary fervour present in the student population and to name any potential revisionists. Mao outlined his tried-and-tested revolutionary agenda to Yuanxin, anticipating, correctly, that his nephew would find them exhilarating and pass them on.

Having lit a fire under the student population, Mao turned to the army. Lin Biao had done a very good job. In 1964, he commissioned the *Quotations of Chairman Mao Zedong*, soon known as the *Little Red Book*, a collection of bite-sized quotes and sayings taken from Mao's work. Every soldier was issued with a copy and made to read it every day until he or she knew it by heart.

In 1965, Lin went further down the pro-Mao line. He stripped soldiers' uniforms of badges or signs of office, creating the guerrilla warrior look that Mao liked so much.

It all came together in Shanghai in 1965. There, a handful of intellectuals followed the Maoist line, led by Zhang Chunqiao, who was to become one of the Gang of Four (see p 100). It became the ideological centre of the Cultural Revolution. The intellectuals targeted

Recipe for revolution

Mao believed that China's young people should carry the revolutionary ideal forward. Remembering that they had not suffered the hardships of his generation, he offered this advice to help them rekindle the flame of rebellion:

- Be a genuine Marxist-Leninist.
- Be willing to serve the masses.
- Accept criticism from the majority however misplaced it seems.
- Be obedient to democratic centralism.
- Be modest and always ready for self-criticism.

▲ The Cultural Revolution affected many areas of Chinese life, in particular the army. This photograph shows the distribution of communist literature to young soldiers in Shanghai.

writers, dramatists, artists, philosophers and historians. Then they moved on to education departments in the party, who supported such artists, and then on to ministers in charge of the departments, gradually working their way up the party hierarchy. In the army, Lin Biao began replacing important military staff with Mao supporters. While not himself engaging in revolution, Mao had created the climate for it. He set in motion one

The *Little Red Book*

This publication was Lin Biao's idea. To keep soldiers on the straight ideological path he put together a small volume, bound in red cloth, containing 33 chapters. Each chapter contains short quotations from a wide range of Mao's writings. The chapters cover every aspect of life. It was published in 1964, with an English-language edition following in 1966. Lin Biao wrote in the preface: "Study Chairman Mao's writings, follow his teachings and act according to his instructions."

The *Little Red Book* was a publishing phenomenon. More than 83 million copies were printed in various editions. It was popular with students in western Europe, who were conducting their own revolution at the time.

of his favourite political games – "let's see you and him fight".

The revolution begins

Until May 1966, the intellectual fighting had taken place within the party, out of the public eye. Then Nie Yuanzi, a friend of Jiang Qing and lecturer in philosophy at Beijing University, put up a "big character" poster denouncing the deputy director and president of the university and the first secretary of the Communist Party in Beijing. Within hours, thousands more posters, written by supporters, had appeared. There was great confusion. Liu Shaoqi and others believed some of the posters were anti-communist and anti-party rather than anti-revisionist and began to counter-attack. But Mao endorsed the poster campaign. He even wrote words of encouragement for the students to put on wall posters – "Make revolution and rebel against any form of authority." *The People's Daily Newspaper* backed the students. The army offered help to the dissidents to study Mao Zedong's Thought.

The movement spread from university to university and into high schools.

▲ *Soldiers of the People's Liberation Army read in unison from Mao's* Little Red Book.

Students began to wear paramilitary uniforms and red armbands, proclaiming themselves the Red Guard, defenders of Mao. They all bought copies of the *Little Red Book*. They were encouraged to attack their revisionist teachers.

And Mao once again showed his mastery of public relations. In July he was photographed swimming smoothly in the Yangtze, showing at once how fit and strong he was, and how unafraid he was of the revolutionary zeal all round him. A month later, he stood on top of

Tiananmen Gate in military uniform, accepting a Red Guard armband and immediately putting it on his left arm. Below him hundreds of thousands of students waved red flags and *Little Red Books*. Mao had succeeded in engineering a "mass movement" then declared his approval of it, as if it had been a spontaneous outburst.

This was the first of many rallies and it attracted millions of people to Beijing.

▲ *By January 1967, when this photograph was taken, Beijing had become a city covered with posters, and the changes wrought by the Cultural Revolution were affecting just about everyone.*

Students were given free rail tickets to travel around the country, spreading the "Red word". It was a triumph for Mao.

Violence in the party and on the streets

Mao had always encouraged destruction. During the first two years of the Cultural Revolution a terrible violence was unleashed.

Within the party, Mao took the chance to get rid of all his enemies, sometimes permanently. The Central Case Examination Group was set up, chaired by the ever-loyal Zhou Enlai. There were 11 members, including Jiang Qing, Kang Sheng and Chen Boda. Their brief was to prove that any charges brought against individuals were correct and to extract confessions. To do this they used torture, interrogation, starvation and sleep deprivation. Well-known party figures underwent the treatment, including Peng Dehuai and, in 1968, Liu Shaoqi. By 1976, when Mao died, almost two million people had been "investigated".

Outside the party, on the streets, the Red Guard were given free reign. Anybody could be denounced for anything – even reading a foreign book. The Red Guard destroyed monuments, museums, libraries, Buddhist temples and works of art. They entered people's houses and workplaces and took anything they considered incriminating – letters, diaries, even books. The only place they could not enter was Mao's private compound, Zhongnanghai, and top-secret installations where the Chinese atomic bomb was being developed. Yet Mao did not intervene when his daughter Li Min spent five months under harsh criticism and his other daughter Li Na was sent to a rectification school.

No one knows how many were killed, or killed themselves, during this period. The Red Guard laid down the law. Their manifesto included banning jeans and "slick hairdos", smoking and drinking for under 35s, and encouraged criticism of elders and teachers. Mao's picture had to be displayed in every house, train, bus, cab and bicycle, and every Chinese person had to carry a copy of the *Little Red Book*. Different groups of Red Guards also fought each other for the right to patrol an area. For

the people, it was like living under the warlords again.

Controlling chaos

Mao was too much of a seasoned politician not to understand what he had unleashed, but he believed he had it under control. With the army on his side, the Red Guard could be easily wiped out if they got out of hand. In August 1966, he wanted to give the students four months – to take to the streets, write big character posters and let foreign journalists take photographs if they wanted to. Yet only two months later, he almost admitted that he had been wrong, and that people might have "bitter words" for him.

Even so, he carried on, as he had with the Great Leap. At the seventh rally of Red Guards in November 1966, he said:

"Long live comrades! You must let politics take command. Go to the masses, and be with the masses. You must conduct the great proletarian Cultural Revolution even better."

◀ Red Guards wore fatigue-style uniforms and red armbands and carried copies of the Little Red Book. Mao-era memorabilia is popular in Chinese shops today, as shown here in this 1997 photo.

Yet behind his man-of-the-people mask, Mao was busy putting the brakes on. Workers were agitating for higher pay and better working conditions and this seemed unacceptable, even to the leftist intellectuals. The workers' groups that were set up to support the revolution were dismantled and their power curbed. The Red Army was overwhelmed by bureaucracy. After the destruction of local government, Mao instructed that new committees should be set up, consisting of the Red Guard, regular army officers and local officials who were politically acceptable. As in any three-way organization, this meant that nothing was ever agreed upon and little progress was made.

The militant period of the revolution was over, but the hunt for revisionists continued until 1976. And Mao's committee solution only worked as a temporary measure. Lin Biao considered that his work with the army had made the Cultural Revolution possible and now he wanted his reward. Jiang Qing began to realize that the Red Guard could form her own power base.

Mao's last moves

Despite increasing ill health, Mao continued in power for another decade after the Cultural Revolution.

Mao's body may have been weakening but his political brain was as sharp as ever. He escaped an assassination attempt in 1971, and foiled the political ambitions of Jiang Qing and Deng Xiaoping. On Zhou Enlai's advice he made successful advances to the west, meeting leaders from the USA and the UK. He also found time to start an anti-Confucius campaign. (Mao had always hated Confucius.) He died in September 1976, at the age of 83.

Lin Biao's plot

Military chief and Minister of Defence Lin Biao was expecting to succeed Mao as China's leader. In fact, he was named as successor at the Ninth Chinese Communist Party Congress in November 1969. However, this may have been a ploy to make him feel secure. Mao had no intention of handing over power to him. Lin had delivered the army into Mao's hands, and now, recognizing Lin's ambition, Mao wanted to get rid of him. Mao knew that many soldiers were

fanatically loyal to Lin, and he did not want to split the army into factions. So, he ordered Zhou Enlai, the persuasive diplomat, to find officers who could be talked into coming on to Mao's side. At the same time, he began to promote Jiang Qing's political career.

Lin suspected that Mao was going to betray him, perhaps as early as 1970. In 1971, he decided to take matters into his own hands. He made a plan, possibly with Soviet backing, to assassinate Mao by blowing up the special train in which he travelled. Then Lin would seize power. But Lin's daughter by his first marriage uncovered the plot and warned Zhou Enlai.

Lin fled, flying out of China (probably to the USSR) with his wife and several others who had been involved in the plot. The plane they were in crashed in Manchuria, and all those on board were killed. The facts about the coup are

▶ *This official photograph of Mao became known worldwide when US artist Andy Warhol used it as the basis for a series of artworks.*

confused. Some sources say that the assassination was planned for 8 August 1971, which means that Lin was free until September. Why and how the plane crashed has never been explained. The Chinese people themselves were not told about the event until 1972.

Jiang Qing and the "Gang of Four"

From 1970 onwards, Jiang began to be more active in public life. Although, by 1973, there was no love lost between her and Mao, he did not oppose her rise to power. She was useful to him, as a focus for the bad feeling that the Cultural Revolution had stirred up. If he could present her in a bad light, he could continue as Beloved Father of the Nation. In public, Mao said that he supported Jiang to encourage more women to take an active part in politics. He was quoted as saying that woman's role in revolution was just as important as man's role. However, it is more likely that he wanted to groom Jiang to carry on his policies, especially his Thought, after his death.

The Gang of Four

During this period Jiang Qing began her rise to political power, after 20 years spent in the background. In Shanghai, she worked with three other leftist radicals – Zhang Chunqiao, Yao Wenyuan and Wang Hongwen. Jiang was the leader of the Gang. They were extremely radical. They controlled the media and used violence as a first resort. All four rose to be members of the Politburo. However, they were arrested after Mao's death when they tried to seize power.

People took notice of what Jiang said because they assumed Mao backed her. Mao encouraged the formation of the Gang of Four – he even gave them their name – because Jiang Qing did not have much political expertise and he thought she needed support. Any remaining Lin Biao sympathizers were purged from the army, and Jiang's connection with it strengthened. One of the Gang of Four, Zhang Chunqiao, was made Director of the Political Department of the army. Mao always believed that revolutionary passion was no use without strong-arm back-up. At the Tenth Party Congress in 1973, the

Gang of Four became members of the Politburo. It seemed clear that Mao intended Jiang and the Gang of Four to be his successors.

But did he? In 1973, Mao reinstated Deng Xiaoping, who was disgraced during the Cultural Revolution and had been working in a tractor factory. Deng and Jiang had always loathed each other. Either Mao had changed his mind about Jiang succeeding him, or, more likely, he was setting up another political game, cancelling out the power of two rivals by setting them against each other.

Mao and the west

While dealing with domestic policy, Mao also began to look outside China. The relationship with the USSR had broken down, and in 1969 fighting had started along the border of the two countries. The war in Vietnam was raging, and the Russians were fighting in North Vietnam, on China's doorstep. Relations with the USA had not been good since the Korean War, but the Americans had made a concession to China. Taiwan (the US-backed nationalist stronghold) lost its seat at

the United Nations, being now considered part of China, and the USA did not object.

Encouraged and advised by Zhou Enlai, Mao now thought it would be a good idea to approach the USA on friendly terms. It would be useful to play the USA off against the USSR. If China were friendly to the USA, the alliance might speed up the end of the Vietnam War. Mao would be seen as a significant figure on the world stage, which would increase his importance at home. Of course, friendship with the west was a complete political U-turn. There had recently been mass demonstrations in China, organized against the decadent western imperialists. Mao had made such turns before, and did not fear any opposition.

Although Zhou Enlai and Deng Xiaoping had travelled all over the world on diplomatic missions, Mao had not been outside China except for one visit to Moscow. Now he was too ill to travel. Negotiations began with Henry Kissinger, the US adviser on national security, who made a secret visit to Beijing in July 1971. Following

▲ *An historic moment – US President Richard Nixon meets Mao Zedong on 18 February 1972.*

this, Richard Nixon, the President of the USA, was invited to China. He was the first foreign head of state to set foot in the People's Republic.

On 18 February 1972, Nixon and Kissinger met Mao in his study at Zhongnanhai for an informal meeting. Mao was physically weak – he had to be helped to stand up and sit down again, and his speech was slurred, but he was friendly and outgoing. He went on to meet Edward Heath, leader of the British Conservative Party in 1974, and US President Gerald Ford in 1975. He made a good impression on the western leaders and their visits resulted in improved trade and cultural links.

Mao's health

All this time, Mao's health was getting worse. His last public appearance was at the May Day celebrations of 1972. It is thought that he may have been suffering from Parkinson's Disease, which explains his slurred speech. Certainly he suffered bouts of pneumonia, had trouble with his teeth, and his eyesight was bad. A month before he met Nixon, he was diagnosed with congestive heart disease and his limbs began to swell up.

Mao now spent much of his time travelling in his special train or staying at various guesthouses in the country. His constant companion was a young woman named Zhang Yufeng. Her job was to read political documents to him and to interpret his speech.

In 1974 he was diagnosed with amyotrophic lateral sclerosis, a form of motor neurone disease also known as Lou Gehrig's disease. The muscles on the right side of his body no longer worked, and he found it difficult to swallow or breathe. He travelled on his train to visit Changsha and Wuhan for the last time.

The anti-Confucius campaign

The thoughts of philosopher Confucius had been the backbone of Chinese society for centuries. Designed by a civil servant for an emperor, it was a traditional, conservative system that respected age, authority and the hierarchy. Everyone knew their place and was expected to stay in it. Women were considered second-class citizens. The Confucian way remained in people's minds despite decades of unrest and the Cultural Revolution. Mao was at one with Emperor Qin Shi Huangdi (259–210 BC), who burnt Confucian books and buried 460 Confucian scholars alive.

Like the Cultural Revolution and the Hundred Flowers Movement, the campaign produced arrests and executions. Mao tried to link it with the disgraced traitor Lin Biao, who was an unpopular public figure because of his attempt to assassinate Mao. If Lin was a Confucianist and a traitor, then Confucianism could not be acceptable. Even Zhou Enlai was criticized during the anti-Confucius campaign, which fizzled out after Mao's death.

He also launched his last act of defiance, the anti-Confucius campaign. In 1975, a cataract operation gave him back some of his sight so that he was able to read again, but by now he was almost paralyzed. His nephew Mao Yuanxin kept him up to date with what was happening on the streets and the Politburo began to hold their meetings in a nearby room.

Last days

At the beginning of 1976 Zhou Enlai had been diagnosed with cancer, and was dying in hospital. Mao was too ill to visit him. After Zhou's death in April, there was a massive demonstration of public mourning in Beijing's Tiananmen Square. The army and police responded violently. Only Jiang Qing or Deng Xiaoping could have authorized such actions. Thinking that Deng was responsible, Mao dismissed him from office again. But he did not leave a clear field for Jiang Qing. In the last surprising move of his career, Mao appointed the little known Hua Guofeng, the party secretary for Mao's home province of Hunan, as his successor, so denying power to both Jiang Qing and the supporters of Deng.

On 11 May 1976, Mao suffered the first of a succession of heart attacks. A second struck on 16 June. He called a meeting of the Politburo, where he spoke of his fears for a future without him. On 2 September Mao Zedong suffered from a third attack, and he died on 9 September 1976.

Mao's achievements

Mao had risen from nothing to be leader of his country. Historians describe him as monster or guru depending on their political attitude. Regardless of his Marxist philosophy, the people treated him as an emperor, and he behaved like one. Although not scholarly, he was a smart, cunning, manipulative and devious master of propaganda – the complete politician. Stubbornly convinced of the rightness of his own ideas, he learned to be inscrutable and to bide his time for maximum impact.

When Mao was born, China had been living under the last remnants of imperial rule, dying under the piecemeal attack of foreign powers. By the time he died, the country had been unified as a People's Republic. Millions had died, but many had seen improvements. China was once again a world power.

▶ *China grieves for its leader. Following Mao's death on 9 September 1976 a mass memorial meeting was held in Tiananmen Square, Beijing.*

Glossary

Comintern An abbreviation of "Communist International", an institution founded in 1919 by the Soviet Communist Party. It was set up to help promote the revolution worldwide.

Communism Political theory. Its main principle is the common ownership of property, wealth and the means of production. It was described by the German thinker Karl Marx in the *Communist Manifesto*.

Communist Manifesto Written by Karl Marx and Friedrich Engels and published in 1848, the *Communist Manifesto* sets out the principles of communism.

Democratic centralism A Marxist-Leninist principle; the proletariat, although necessary for revolution, are politically ill-equipped to rule. The Communist Party is seen as a direct representative of the proletariat, and therefore has the power to rule in its name.

Dogmatic deviation Having a different opinion (to the Thought of Chairman Mao) based on the dogma of a different political theory.

Empiricist deviation Having a different opinion (to the Thought of Chairman Mao) based on new thoughts of your own.

Five Year Plan An idea introduced in the USSR by Stalin in 1928 to modernize the economy. The plans were meant to reorganize farming along industrial lines, and to transform Russia from an agricultural to a manufacturing economy.

Marx, Karl (1818–83) German thinker, writer and economist. He co-wrote the *Communist Manifesto* (1848) and *Das Kapital*, the first volume of which was published in 1867, but which he never finished. His philosophy was taken up by Vladimir Illych Lenin, leader of the Russian revolution, and used as the theoretical basis of political action in the USSR.

Marxism Communism according to Karl Marx. Marx believed that communism would be created when the working classes revolted against the ruling elite. This action would get rid of class distinctions and end exploitation of the many by the few. Each person would contribute to society according to his or her abilities, and each would receive according to his or her needs. Society would be fair, everything would be shared in common. Crime would become irrelevant. Over time, government would become unnecessary.

Marxism-Leninism Marxism interpreted by Lenin, leader of the Russian revolution of 1917. It did not agree with direct rule by the proletariat, because the workers were considered politically uneducated. Instead, it introduced the idea of democratic centralism. Maoism was based on Marxism-Leninism.

Proletariat Term for the working classes.

Treaty ports Ports in Imperial China signed over to foreign countries. The European country to which they were conceded was allowed to build a consulate and appoint a Resident (an official with legal powers). Foreign nationals were allowed to live there under the laws of their own country. In effect, they were little pieces of the home country within China. Shanghai and Guangzhou were both important treaty ports. Chinese people living in and around treaty ports picked up western ideas, and many Chinese students travelled from treaty ports to study abroad.

Who's who

Until 1949, the standard system used to convert Chinese pictograms into English was called the Wade-Giles romanization system. In the 1950s, the Chinese introduced a new system called pinyin. This means that names and places sometimes have different spellings. For instance Mao Zedong was written as Mao Tse-Tung and Beijing was written Peking.

Some writers use the Wade-Giles system to spell the names of people who have died and pinyin for the names of people who are still alive. Other writers use the Wade-Giles system if they are writing about events and people before 1949 and the pinyin system for the period after 1949. This list shows the pinyin form today in bold, with older versions in roman type. You may find the older names in older books.

Cai Heshen Tsai Ho-shen Mao's best friend at Changsha Normal School. Died in 1931.

Chen Boda Chen Po-ta Theoretician; helped Mao formulate his *Thought*.

Chen Duxiu Chen Tu-hsui One of the two founders of the Communist Party in China.

Chen Shaoyu Chen Shao-yu The other name for Wang Ming, one of Mao's political rivals.

Cixi Tz'u Hsi Last empress of China.

Deng Xiaoping Teng Hsiao-ping Secretary General of the Chinese Communist Party and head of state after Mao's death.

He Zizhen Ho Tzu-chen Mao's third partner.

Hua Guofeng Hua Kuo-feng Mao's successor.

Jiang Jieshi Chiang Kai Shek Leader of the Nationalist Party.

Jiang Qing Chiang Ching Mao's fourth partner.

Li Dazhao Li Ta chao One of the two founders of the Chinese Communist Party.

Lin Biao Lin Piao Mao's minister of defence in the 1960s; planned to assassinate Mao.

Liu Shaoqi Liu Shao-chi Head of State apppointed by Mao in 1959.

Mao Anqing Mao An-Ching Mao's second son.

Mao Anying Mao An-ying Mao's eldest son.

Mao Shunsheng Mao Shun-sheng Mao's father.

Mao Zedong Mao Tse-tung.

Mao Zemin Mao Tse-min Mao's younger brother.

Mao Zetan Mao Tse-tan Mao's youngest brother.

Nie Yuanzi Nieh Yuan-tzu Philosophy lecturer and friend of Jiang Qing.

Peng Dehuai Peng Teh-huai Mao's greatest general and disgraced Minister of Defence.

Qin Shi Huangdi Ch'in Shi-huang Founder of the Qing Dynasty and creator of the first unified Chinese Empire.

Sun Zhongshan/Yixian Sun Yat Sen Founder of the Nationalist Party; established the republic of China.

Wen Qimei Wen Chi-mei Mao's mother.

Yang Changji Yang Chang-chi One of Mao's teachers; father of Yang Kaihui.

Yang Kaihui Yang Kai-hui Mao's second partner.

Zhang Chunqiao Chang Chin-chiao One of the Gang of Four.

Zhang Guotao Chang Kuo-ytao Early communist leader who quarrelled with Mao during the Long March and defected to the nationalists.

Zhang Xueliang Chang Hsueh-liang Warlord who allied with the communists; kidnapped Jiang Jieshi.

Zhou Enlai Chou En-lai Diplomat and tactician; loyal supporter of Mao; never persecuted or put out of office.

Zhu De Chu Teh One of the founders of the People's Liberation Army.

Timeline

1893 Mao Zedong is born in the village of Shaoshan, Hunan province, China on 26 December.

1901 Mao goes to the village school and works on his father's farm.

1908 Mao marries Luo Li; it is an arranged marriage.

1910 Mao attends Tungshan Primary School, against his father's will.

1911 Mao goes to Changsha, the capital of Hunan, and enrols at Xiangxiang Middle School; in October he joins the army.

1912 Mao leaves the army and goes to Hunan First Middle School in Changsha.

1913 Mao trains as a teacher at Hunan First Normal School.

1918 Mao graduates and moves to Beijing; he gets a job in the university library and meets Chen Duxiu and Li Tachao, the founders of the Chinese Communist Party.

1919 Mao goes to Shanghai and then back to Changsha where he becomes active in local politics; Mao's mother dies.

1920 Mao becomes headmaster of Hunan First Normal School's primary school. He sets up home with Yang Kaihui. Mao's father dies.

1921 Mao is one of the 13 people who meet in Shanghai to set up the Chinese Communist Party.

1922 Mao and Yang Kaihui's first son, Anying, is born in October.

1923 Mao elected to the Central Committee of the Chinese Communist Party; his second son, Anqing, is born in November.

1925 Sun Zhongshan, leader of the Nationalist Party (Guomindang), dies. Mao becomes Director of the Guomindang's Training Institute for the Peasant Movement and Secretary of the Guomindang Central Propaganda Department.

1926 Mao becomes Secretary of the Chinese Communist Party's Advisory Committee for the Peasant Movement.

1927 Mao sets up Peasant Training Institute in Wuchang. The alliance between the communists and the Guomindang is split when Jiang Jieshi takes over as nationalist leader. Mao's third son, Anlong, is born. Mao loses all his party posts.

1928 Mao moves to a base in the Jinggang mountains. He sets up home with He Zizhen.

1929 Mao and his supporters set up the Jiangxi Soviet. He and He Zizhen have a son, Anhong.

1930 Mao is under attack from the Communist Party because of his guerrilla warfare tactics. He attacks Changsha but is defeated by the nationalists. Yang Kaihui is shot by the nationalists because she is a communist.

1931 Mao meets Zhou Enlai.

1932 Mao is criticized, loses political and military power and is forced to live in exile in the countryside. The Communist Party moves its headquarters from Shanghai to Jiangxi.

1934 Mao is re-elected as Chairman of the Soviet Central Government. The Long March starts. Mao's brother, Zemin, is killed.

1935 The Zunyi Conference. Mao becomes chairman of the Military Committee. Mao quarrels with other military leaders. He leads his troops to Shaanxi in the north-west. The Long March ends in October.

1936 Jiang Jieshi is kidnapped. Nationalists and communists try to unite against the invading Japanese. Mao and He Zizhen's daughter, Li Min, is born.

1937 Mao moves his headquarters to Yan'an. War breaks out between China and Japan. The nationalists and communists co-operate. Mao sets up home with Jiang Qing. Chen Boda arrives in Yan'an.

1939 World War Two breaks out.

1940 Mao and Jiang Qing's daughter, Li Na, is born.

1942 Mao launches the *Cheng Feng* Movement ("Rectification of Work Theory") to get rid of his political opponents.

1945 Mao is elected Chairman of the Central Committee of the Chinese Communist Party. His political thought is written into the Constitution as the guiding principle of the party. World War Two ends and Germany surrenders. The USA drops atomic bombs on Hiroshima and Nagasaki, and Japan surrenders. Russia declares war on Japan and invades Manchuria.

1946 Despite Mao and Jiang Jieshi signing a peace agreement, fighting breaks out between communists and nationalists.

1947 Mao launches an offensive against the nationalists.

1948 Communists take Manchuria.

1949 Communists take Beijing and Nanjing. In October, Mao announces the formation of the People's Republic of China, with Beijing as the capital. Mao visits Stalin in Moscow.

1950 Mao sends Chinese troops to fight on the North Korean side in the Korean War. His son Anying is killed in the fighting.

1951 Mao introduces thought remoulding movements to ensure his continuing power.

1954 Mao elected as Chairman of the State.

1957 Mao launches "A Hundred Flowers" movement.

1958 The "Great Leap Forward" is launched. Mao resigns as Chairman of the State in December.

1961 Conflict arises between China and the Soviet Union.

1964 Lin Biao publishes the *Little Red Book* containing a collection of quotations from Mao's works.

1966 Mao launches the Cultural Revolution.

1971 Mao orders Lin Biao to be removed from power.

1972 Mao meets US President Nixon in Beijing.

1973 Mao launches the anti-Confucius campaign. His health gets worse.

1976 Mao dies on 9 September.

Further reading

The Rants, Raves and Thoughts of Mao Zedong: The Dictator in His Own Words and Those of Others
Paul Choi (ed.)
On Your Own Publications 2002

Mao Zedong
Christine Hatt
Evans Brothers 2000

Mao's Children in the New China
Yarog Jiang and David Ashley (editors)
Routledge 2000

Mao Zedong's Posters
Cheung Chung Yau, Orville Schell
Odyssey Publications Ltd 2000

Mao Zedong
Jonathan Spence
Weidenfeld & Nicholson 1999

Mao Zedong
Delia Davin
Sutton Publishing 1997

Mao Zedong: Founder of the People's Republic of China
Rebecca Stefoff
Millbrook Press 1996

Index

References shown in italic are pictures or maps.